Let
Buster
Lead

Praise for *Let Buster Lead*

"I'm not a dog person, but I became just as emotionally involved reading about Buster, in Deborah Dozier Potter's memoir *Let Buster Lead*, as I did as a youth reading Alfred Payson Terhune's books about his collie, Lad. He became a person. I felt for him. I cheered for him. I ultimately grieved for him. Buster is a dog who truly made a difference during his life, and Mrs. Potter's love for her subject matter illuminates each page."

—Dominick Dunne

"Deborah Potter vividly elucidates a much under diagnosed illness affecting an estimated 6 to 7 percent of the U.S. population at any one time. As a physician I have witnessed first hand how Post-Traumatic Stress Disorder can destroy families and relationships. I strongly recommend this book to my colleagues and to those who desire a first person account of this illness and its manifestations.

—David A. Gonzales, MD, Inpatient Medicine Program Director, Albuquerque, NM

"*Let Buster Lead* is a love story that begins in the pound, but the adopted pup is beyond ordinary. He rescues a woman who falls prey to a devastating and seemingly incurable illness and saves a marriage in the process. You will weep for joy and heartbreak in the course of reading about this creature, who must be gamboling in heaven with Lassie and Rin Tin Tin and every other legendary dog in literature."

—Sylvia Chase, television news correspondent (20/20, PRIMETIME and NOW on PBS.)

"*Let Buster Lead* is a powerful and compelling story. Those suffering with Post-Traumatic Stress Disorder as well as their family members will enhance their own healing through this warm, honest, and poignant story. The book is a touching and vivid reminder to us all of our hidden inner struggles and can give hope to the many who learn that their recovery will be through relationships—of all kinds! Potter writes in a warm, open and easy personal style; this is a story of courage and commitment."

—Marilyn J. Mason, Ph.D., former family psychologist and celebrity author of *Facing Shame: Families in Recovery* and *Seven Mountains: The Inner Climb to Commitment and Caring*

"Hats off to a talented new writer Deborah Potter. In her first book she spins a touching, charming, altogether winning love story, the likes of which has never been told quite so tenderly before. It will lift your spirits and make you feel good about the world at a time when we need it most."

—Robert Osborne, host of Turner Classic Movies

Let Buster Lead

*My Discovery of Love,
PTSD, and Self-Acceptance*

Deborah Dozier Potter

SUNSTONE
PRESS

SANTA FE

Sunstone books may be purchased for educational, business, or sales promotional use. For information please write: Special Markets Department, Sunstone Press, P.O. Box 2321, Santa Fe, New Mexico 87504-2321.

Book and cover design › Vicki Ahl
Body typeface › Book Antiqua
Printed on acid-free paper
∞
eBook 978-1-61139-340-8

Library of Congress Cataloging-in-Publication Data

Potter, Deborah Dozier.
 Let Buster lead : discovering love, post-traumatic stress disorder and self-acceptance / by Deborah Dozier Potter.
 p. cm.
 ISBN-13: 978-0-86534-591-1 (hardcover : alk. paper)
 1. Potter, Deborah Dozier--Mental health. 2. Post-traumatic stress disorder--Patients--New Mexico--Biography. 3. Dogs--Therapeutic use. I. Title.
 RC552.P67.P685 2007
 616.85'210092--dc22
 [B]
 2007019351

Let Buster lead : my discovery of love, ptsd, and self-acceptance
ISBN: 978-1-63293-038-5 (softcover : alk. paper)

WWW.SUNSTONEPRESS.COM
SUNSTONE PRESS / POST OFFICE BOX 2321 / SANTA FE, NM 87504-2321 /USA
(505) 988-4418 / ORDERS ONLY (800) 243-5644 / FAX (505) 988-1025

If you're a fellow pet owner who has been blessed with the greatest pet who ever lived, the love of your life, this is dedicated to you.

Preface

I learned a lot about myself after my injuries. But I might never have grown from them, had it not been for Buster. Wanting him near me made me discover I had an illness. The therapy I received helped me heal a lot of old emotional fears and pain. Without that support, and his love, going through life with a disability could have changed me into an angry, bitter recluse. Instead, the experience led me to see the kindness in others and the beauty in my own soul. But I still had a lot to learn about myself, and about life, from my best friend.

The story you're about to read is true, and the way I remember it. It isn't an ordinary dog's tale. If something I say offends anyone, my memory isn't perfect.

Discovering One Another

I was still in mourning when I met him. His penetrating brown eyes seemed to beseech my husband and me, telling us he wanted to be anywhere but in cage twenty-six. Our Old English Sheepdog puppy had just died, and we needed a companion for his lonely mother. I felt devastated by another death in our family, and was angry at the Universe (my term for the Powers that hold life together). I had vowed to never let myself love a new person or pet again. But we needed a good companion for Thundercloud. This was going to be her dog, not mine.

So that my husband, Earl, Thundercloud and I could get a better look at "number twenty-six," an animal shelter volunteer brought him out of his cage and into the building's inner courtyard. Our interview with the dog went well. Thundercloud liked the guy. His black and white face was

handsome, and he seemed kind. His perkiness made her happy, and she wagged her stumpy tail when he retrieved the tennis ball we tossed for him. The young dog's gentle smile let us know he liked us, so I hugged him to see if he was affectionate. He put his paws around my neck, then looked me in the eye. He was testing me, as well.

The shelter's manager said our choice was "about a year and a half old," and a "very nice dog." A control officer had found him running loose in a family neighborhood. He wore no license or i.d. tags, just a chain choke collar. "How much land do you have around your house?" the manager asked us. We told him. Then he asked, "Is it fenced in?"

I assumed he wanted our assurance that the dog was going to have enough space for playing and would never be found wandering the streets again. Our barbed wire fencing wasn't dog proof, but no pet of ours had ever run away. Before I could assure him, Earl answered for us. "Yes," he said. "We have a fence. Around our entire property."

The manager was pleased, but he wouldn't let us take our new friend home yet. To allow the dog's owner time to find him, Santa Fe law required the shelter to keep him three more days.

Before the shelter opened on that fourth morning, Earl rushed out of our house like a first-time father, proud to claim his handsome new son.

I was amused and supportive, but too sad to care much. My son and my stepson had finished college, and I was looking forward to less responsibility, not more. And grief still consumed me because my father had died ten months earlier. He was William Dozier, a popular retired film and television producer, best known for the "camp" *Batman*

series. I adored him. I missed his dazzling wit and his deep love for me. Whenever I thought of him, my eyes welled with tears. And only a week had passed since the veterinary surgeon called from Albuquerque to tell me they "couldn't save" Russell, our two-year-old, home born puppy.

As I watched Earl's car race out of our driveway, I remembered hearing Russell's squeal, remembered rushing outside, then seeing him pinned under the front wheel of a delivery truck. I relived the week we spent visiting him at our local vet's, hoping his broken pelvis was healing. I remembered his moans, all night, when we brought him home, and the X-rays at the Albuquerque surgeon's office, showing the broken left thigh our vet had missed. Worst of all, I remembered putting Russell in one of the vet's cages, looking into his eyes and promising him he was going to be all right, then driving sixty miles back to Santa Fe without him. Then the phone call the next morning. "While we were pinning that leg, a blood clot went into his system. We're doing everything possible." Then, the second call. "We're very sorry, Ma'am, but...."

With these memories surging through me, I wrapped my arms around Thundercloud, and cried. Then I walked away from the window and started to dress for a fundraising luncheon.

While putting on make-up, I felt even lower. My churning maternal emotions evoked memories of my own mother, the forties-era movie star Joan Fontaine. She was accomplished and beautiful, but whenever I scrutinized my face in the mirror I would feel dejected by how dull everything about me was, compared to her. She so often told me as a child that I was never going to be pretty or ambitious enough

to be a successful actress, never witty enough to be the social star she was, never focused enough to read as many books as she had. Eye shadow and mascara weren't helping me that morning. My eyes were red and puffy.

A phone call from my husband lifted my mood. He told me "twenty-six" had greeted him with a smile and a wagging tail, had stood still while the adoption papers were signed, then hopped into the car. "I know we're disappointed in our vet," he said. "But the shelter told me to take him for shots. So, I took him there. They let us in right away." He said the seasoned old veterinarian gave the dog his required vaccines, then discovered he had already been neutered. "Twenty-six" was about eighteen months old, weighed forty pounds, was still growing, and seemed in good health. But he was underfed, and very thin. "I got his license and an i.d. tag," Earl added. "We're on our way home, almost in the driveway."

"Could they tell what breed he is?" I asked.

"I forgot ask to about that. I was too excited. Next time."

The dog's first moments in our house were disastrous. Earl let him in through the kitchen door. He ran straight to our bedroom, then lunged at my beloved cat, Wrex. When I embraced the hissing kitty, his claws shredded my silk blouse. Then the cat leapt out of my arms, flew behind the living room sofa and hid there, petrified.

"Wrex, honey, come out," I said. "Come and meet the new doggie. Let's try again."

Wrex hissed, and he wouldn't move.

Thundercloud looked at me. She seemed to be amused.

During the next few days we let everyone bond. Our skinny new puppy came when he was called, was house-broken and didn't chew furniture. He and Thundercloud seemed very comfortable together. But whenever Wrex entered a room, "skinny" crouched down and glared at him, curling his lip to display his sharp canine teeth. To teach the new dog that this behavior was unacceptable, Earl and I banished him from our "pack" by shutting him out of the room. In five minutes, we let him return. After a few of those lessons, he stopped stalking the cat. "Good boy." Big smile. "Smart boy." Wagging tail.

He also made us earn his respect. Politeness was essential. When we spoke to him in an angry tone, he trembled and shrank away. He recoiled if we reached out to his face too quickly. If his tail was touched, he snapped at us. To me, these reactions were obvious signs of physical and emotional abuse. *Someone must have hurt him over a long period of time*, I said to myself. *Poor little guy. I hope he ran away.*

He wanted to be understood. Those brown eyes seemed to talk to us, asking us to do things for him. With a prance and a toss of his head, he showed us when and where he wanted us to follow him. He was a little cocky and very smart, so we decided to name him Buster.

We weren't smart enough to know he was training us. My awareness of the lessons he taught came much later.

He and Thundercloud played well together. With his mouth, Buster often grabbed some of her shaggy, silver fur, and she didn't seem to mind. Soon, Wrex clearly loved being stalked by him. The little cat flirted with Buster. He ogled him, over his slinky black shoulder, inviting him on

streaking chases throughout the house. Often, they would stare at one another for several minutes, each daring the other to flinch.

Wrex loved Buster's attention and Thundercloud liked having some company. But we couldn't understand why the new dog didn't stay home. Every day, he left the house for hours. *We like him,* I told myself. *But, maybe he doesn't like us. He'll either stay here, or he won't. Don't let yourself get attached to him.* I had learned that life was unpredictable and not always fair.

One afternoon a woman phoned me at my office "on behalf of a beautiful black and white dog." Buster had followed two bicyclists home, and they were kind enough to keep him tethered until I picked him up. Their house was over a mile away from ours, and I felt hurt by his defection.

While Buster sat in my car's passenger seat, I had a little talk with him. "Why were you following those people?" I asked. "Don't we amuse you enough?"

Nose in the air.

"Don't we feed you enough?"

Head down. Bashful glance.

"You rascal!"

Then he butted the window with his nose. I pressed the window button and opened it for him. He sniffed the passing scenery the rest of the way home. We had talked enough.

One Saturday night I was sure we had lost him. It was almost midnight, and he had been gone since noon. Feeling close to frantic, Earl phoned the animal shelter. Buster was there! He wore a bright red collar, with tags, but nobody had called us.

When Earl brought Buster home, they were both smiling and they looked exhausted. "I rushed through the door of the shelter," Earl told me. "As soon as I said hello to the guy behind the desk, I heard this screeching howl from back where the cages are. Buster must have recognized my voice! When they brought him out, he skidded across the linoleum floor and jumped into my arms." While Earl was talking, I watched Buster curl up under the kitchen table. He heaved a deep sigh, then went to sleep.

Early the next Saturday morning, we couldn't find Buster. *Where did he go? Is he looking for something?* There was nothing we could do but wait. When he returned through the dog flap that afternoon, I was delighted to see him. He had found his way back from wherever he had been. I knew he had decided our house was his home. We were his family by choice.

"Welcome home," I said.

I reached out to hug him but he trotted right past me.

"Yeah, yeah," he seemed to say. "It's time for my nap."

Now that he had really decided to live with us, I decided to provide more fun. Late one afternoon, we played catch with the tennis ball, then I threw a Frisbee for him. He didn't retrieve it; he just stared at it. He seemed to have no idea what to do.

I threw it a few times, telling him to catch it. His eyes told me I looked like an idiot. In that sing-song voice we adults use for toddlers and dogs, I said, "Catch the Frisbee. See? Frisbee, Frisbee! Catch!" He gave me a puzzled look,

lay down on the grass, and crossed his paws. Then he nosed his tennis ball and stared at me.

I went inside, and returned with some butter. When I gave him a taste, he liked it. He also liked licking it off my fingers. I rubbed some butter on the Frisbee, then held it in front of his nose. He tasted the butter. "Good boy." I tossed the Frisbee a few feet away. He went to it, then looked at me, still puzzled. "It's okay." My own adult voice seemed to assure him. He licked the Frisbee. "Good boy." I added more butter, and threw the Frisbee. He picked it up, and brought it back to me. "Good boy! Good boy!!" We repeated this, without the butter, until he was chasing the Frisbee halfway across the lawn and sailing five feet into the air to catch it. He brought it back each time, eager to fetch it again. I couldn't wait to tell Earl, "We have a Frisbee dog!"

A delightful dance had begun. That Saturday, Earl and Buster played Frisbee for almost an hour, both adoring their new game. Buster soared into the air, made his catch, then pranced back with his prize. Even when the corners of his mouth were bloody, he crouched down, tail in the air, eyes open wide, asking for more. After we bought a soft Frisbee, this play became their evening ritual, even in the dark. Dogs can easily hear what they can't see.

Buster continued to impress me. He was a hard worker, had an untiring will to please and a sweet nature. I was glad he was part of our family, even though I still felt blue about Russell. At two, Russell had been a huge dog who didn't even obey his mother. Buster's size and personality were better for us and better for Thundercloud. He was a blessing. We had found a wonderful dog.

But he continued to leave home for hours. These ab-

sences concerned us, because Thundercloud was left alone to protect the house. Buster was very sweet with her, they never fought, and they seemed to be good friends. Earl and I were baffled. "Why doesn't he stay home? What is he looking for?"

We never heard a complaint from a neighbor, and Buster always returned. A loud whistle usually brought him back in five minutes, so we bought a battery-operated bullhorn to make our whistles louder. We didn't let his absences worry us; he was our "wandering wolf."

Maybe he was part wolf, Earl and I speculated. We had never seen a dog like him. His black and white fur was thick, not long. His markings looked like a tuxedo and white gloves. His head and legs looked a little wolfish, but the wide white stripe down his adorable black face seemed pure family pet. Yet, like a wolf, he adored being in the wild.

The first time we took him hiking with friends, we climbed to a high forest lake. Exhausted, we sat on the shore with Thundercloud and our friends' dog. Across the lake, we saw a creature dive into the water and swim after something. We were frightened, until the creature turned out to be Buster. "Great dog," our friends exclaimed. "What kind of dog is he? Is he part wolf?" We wondered what talents he would show us next.

* * *

No matter how much they amused us, we usually left our pets alone at home. During our first decade of marriage, Earl and I had spent each weekday and evening at his tiny law firm. His specialty was real estate and business law, so

we sat through countless, intense nighttime public hearings. I had been a "Hollywood" agent when I found absolute passion with Earl, a handsome divorcé. After I married Earl and moved to his home in Santa Fe, I worked as agent-manager-publicist for a successful film actor. I also managed Earl's law firm facility, and helped organize fundraising events for the opera, the orchestra and several political candidates. My husband and I made time to be loving parents to his two young sons. His adopted son, Cody, was seven when we married, and he lived with us. Soon I became that adorable child's adoptive mother. As a couple, Earl and I thrived on stress, faith in the Universe, and our passion for one another.

By the time we met Buster, Earl and I had been married thirteen years, the actor had left me for other agents, the law firm had expanded into a second building, our sons were starting their own lives on both coasts, and we were partners in a hotel development company. We went to business gatherings most nights and traveled constantly. We were delegates to three national political conventions, we visited our sons when they let us, and we nurtured old friendships in Los Angeles and New York. On warm weekends at home, we took our dogs hiking.

When we were away, the manager of a local restaurant often stayed in our house with the pets. Each time we dined at that restaurant, the waiters would tell us they loved playing Frisbee with Buster. We got great service, an occasional free Margarita, and were glad to know our little "family" had good care.

Once, when we went to one of Earl's family reunions in Quogue, Long Island, his cousins invited us to play golf.

We had both grown up considering golf to be a folly for obtuse, wealthy men. But, to our guilty astonishment, we enjoyed it. We swallowed our presumptions and decided it was "hiking with something to do." About a year later, we made time for lessons.

One spring day, I was hitting yellow plastic practice balls on our lawn at home. To my delight, Buster retrieved each ball for me. "Good boy." When I hit the ball, he would bring it back. His happy expression told me he loved doing this job. So, I tried a real golf ball, sending it into the piñon and juniper trees beyond the lawn. He ran after it, then turned and looked at me, bewildered.

"I can't find that thing," he seemed to say. "I can't see it. It's too fast to hear, and it doesn't have a scent."

When I hit another real ball, he still didn't run after it. Instead, he sat down next to me, and watched me work. Being around work seemed to fascinate him. That August, Earl and I learned why. We stopped at our county's fair when they were having "sheepdog demonstrations." Since Thundercloud was a sheepdog, we thought we might enjoy the event. What we discovered was surprising.

2

Becoming Best Friends

As we sat in the bleachers watching the sheepdogs work, the announcer explained what they were doing. At the start of each round, a dog and its handler entered the arena. Next, a small flock of sheep was let in. The dog didn't bark at the sheep or nip at their heels the way Old English Sheepdogs herd. The dog stayed quiet and did a slithery dance around the flock. Then the dog crouched down and pranced toward the sheep, glaring at them to get them to move. The intimidated sheep walked through gates and into pens as the dog circled them.

Most of the dogs were black. The tips of their long tails were white, their lower legs were white, and they had white neck and chest fur. They looked like they were wearing tuxedoes.

"These Border Collies," the announcer explained,

"originate from the border between Scotland and England. They're considered to be the most intelligent breed among all dogs. Most of these dogs are still working when they're twelve years old, and they often live well past fifteen. They're very popular here in northern New Mexico because we have so many sheep farms. They herd with their eyes, not their bark. They protect their herd by circling it and defending its border. Most Border Collies have a two-mile radius, called a 'fetch.' They consider the fetch their territory. To protect the herd, they patrol their territory. They make good pets, but they are working dogs and must be kept occupied. If not, they'll try to herd whatever they can, even cars. They must have a job. They thrive on work.

"You can tell a good Border Collie herder by they way they crouch and glare when they herd, and..."

"That's it," Earl said. "Buster's a Border Collie! He even looks like these dogs."

We realized Buster didn't stalk Wrex for fun. He was herding him. When he left home, he was patrolling the neighborhood, working to protect us. Most likely, he was looking for a job.

Then we shared thoughts about how Buster behaved when we went hiking. In the forest he was seldom in front of us, or behind. That's where Thundercloud walked. Buster ran in and out of the woods, crossing the path several times, circling us. He hiked four miles for every one of ours.

He *did* thrive on work. All his instincts told him to protect us. We were his herd. He devoted himself to any job we gave him. We had been too busy to notice. Suddenly, so much about Buster made sense.

We drove home from the fairgrounds, and called him with the bullhorn. Soon he was prancing toward us, smiling.

When I looked at him, I saw a different Buster. He wasn't just the good-hearted Frisbee dog, he was someone I finally understood. I wanted to apologize for three years of ignorance. When I knelt down and hugged him, he nuzzled his cheek against mine. I think he already knew what I was going to say.

"I'm so sorry, B," I told him. "We were too dumb to know you were protecting us all this time. We need to give you more to do. I'm very sorry."

When I stood up, he wagged his tail. Then he rose up on his hind legs and put his front paws on my shoulders. We hugged again. After that, he nudged me with his nose, telling me he wanted to play.

From then on, Earl threw the Frisbee for him twice a day. When our son, Cody, moved back to Santa Fe, he and his friends came to the house and played Frisbee with Buster. When the weather was too cold for hiking, Earl and I took both dogs for walks in town. Buster liked a long leash so he could greet people before they came near us, giving them ample time to stop and admire him.

"He's gorgeous," the women usually said. "What's his name?"

"Great dog," said the men. "I want one like that. What kind is he?"

Twice, people who identified themselves as Border Collie breeders asked where he was bred. They were astonished to learn we had found him at the pound. They complimented us on his large size, his uniform markings

and strong conformation. Buster loved the attention.

But his straying away continued to worry me. One evening, he came home with lipstick on his face. A florescent pink mouth print, smack on the middle of it. *The nerve of some woman!* I felt jealous. To deserve the love of this beautiful creature, I decided to do more to keep him. But I didn't know how I was going to find the time.

By then, I was helping Earl hold his law firm together. He didn't have enough time for his clients or his staff. He had been elected chairman of a state political party, and I expected myself to be his adoring partner through every activity. There were constant meetings, receptions, fundraisers, and a presidential election to prepare for. I was also on the board of a local college and had been appointed to one boards of the Kennedy Center in Washington. My husband and I both traveled several times a month. Our phone rang from dawn to midnight.

In less than a year I watched Earl's sunny personality become subdued, as though he was wearing a stiff layer of armor around himself that kept a swarm of emotions at bay. I also watched him take my companionship for granted. I felt exhausted and depressed. The pressures and commitments erased all our private time, straining our affection for one another.

But Buster wanted my affection. Each time I got ready to lie down, even for a nap, he pranced ahead of me, eager to lead me to the bed. "I'll be right there," I often explained. As soon as I put my head on the pillow, I would feel his nose lifting my hand. Then I would tap my other hand on the

comforter, asking him to jump on board. He sailed up onto the bed, then nestled down next to me. As we lay together, he rested his head on my chest. Sometimes we curled up like spoons, and slept.

I spent less time at the office. Afternoons at home, alone with my dogs and Wrex, helped me cope with my intense political and business nightlife. In social arenas, I was poised, gregarious and diplomatic on the surface, but my emotions were churning underneath. I took antidepressants, but all that "keeping busy" did nothing to mask my loneliness. I loved having dinner with Cody once a week, but the pressures of being a state chairman's wife kept growing. I missed being able to phone my father; I needed his astute advice about dealing with people. When someone would phone to criticize Earl, demand his time, or grab a last minute interview, I was afraid of what I might say. So the answering machine took messages, and my pets loved me no matter how I felt.

I couldn't hide my feelings from Buster. He understood me. When I cried, he put his head on my lap. When I needed a hug, he gave me one. When I was exhausted, he lay down on the bed and licked my face. When I was angry, he ran out of the house. When I was happy, he was prancy and playful. When I went jogging, he followed. If I scolded him and ordered him back to the house, he headed toward home. Then he would follow at a distance, trying to hide behind trees. He wanted to protect me from passing cars.

And he would not be fooled. I could never lie to him. Whenever I took him to our new veterinary clinic and told him "this won't hurt," he trembled and tried to climb onto

my lap. When I admitted, "They're going to give you a little poke today," he was calm.

I usually had his full attention. Unless he was sleeping, he watched me, always aware of what I was doing. If I sat in a room, he lay down, facing the exit. When I stood, he stood, ready to lead me. When I focused on a project he lay still, usually with his front paws crossed, but his eyes stayed on me. If I made a quick trip from one room to another, he stayed still. He knew how soon I would return, even if I didn't know myself. When I wasn't going to return in a few seconds, he followed me into that room. When I went from room to room, so did he. Even into the bathroom. Outside, I snapped my fingers to get his attention. A simple nod of the head in a certain direction told him to move that way.

He smiled when I smiled at him. To laugh with me, he opened his mouth very wide. He talked, too. I didn't know what he was saying, but some expressions were obvious. Loud panting from the back seat of the car meant, "Open the window." Three loud, throaty pants meant, "I'm right here." A slight whine meant, "Pay attention to me." Wriggling and whining a little meant he was very happy and excited. A low growl said, "Don't do that." A big yawn, ending in a long squeal meant, "Hello" or "I just woke up from a nap. What are we going to do now?" A gliding scratch on the door, light as a harp strum, meant, "Open the door, I want to see you." When he moved his tongue in and out, it was a request for his evening cookie. Lifting my hand with a light nudge of his nose was asking for love.

But lifting my hand with a sharp push meant "come with me, right away." Once he had my attention, he wriggled his body, and faced in the direction he wanted me to

follow. He wanted me to go outside, play with the Frisbee, or open a door for Thundercloud.

Even though Earl fed him each morning, Buster stayed by my side the rest of the time. He followed me to my car, wanting to go to the office with me. When I wore high heels or ski clothes, he didn't follow. He knew I was going someplace I couldn't take him. If I stayed out all day, he was seldom home when I returned. He was working someplace else.

3

The Girlfriend

That summer, Earl and I attended all the political meetings and pre-conventions before the national convention, then the convention itself. After three exhausting months, I only went to events I thought I might enjoy. One of those was the annual parade in a mountain village. We love the people there, and being in their parade gave me a chance to indulge my childhood passion: riding a horse.

On the way, we stopped in another village to see friends who own a sheep ranch. Just before dinner, their youngest daughter placed a Border Collie puppy in my hands.

"Do you want one?" she asked. "Daddy says we have to give this litter away. We have too many dogs."

Buster needs a playmate, I told myself. *Thundercloud isn't*

as smart as he is. A puppy might amuse him and keep him home.

Earl and I asked our friends to select a female for us and save her until she was weaned. We promised to return for her.

In mid-September, the little girl's mother returned my phone calls. She said they had been away moving sheep, but had saved a puppy for us. "She's adorable. She has the cutest face. We're all falling in love with her." That Sunday, we drove our dogs up to the ranch to bring the puppy home.

When I got out of the car, Thundercloud stayed in the back seat, but Buster jumped out. He rushed over to a truck filled with sheep, and stared at them. I think it was his first encounter with sheep. We didn't want all the dogs in the area excited, so I firmly asked him to get back into the car.

I walked over to the house, and saw Earl caressing a ball of black fluff. His expression told me everything: he was in love. The puppy had melted his armor.

We sat on the porch with our friends and watched the tiny fluff ball scamper behind her mother. She followed her around the ranch, wriggling under fences when Mom sailed over them. When it was time to leave, we put the puppy in the car with Buster and Thundercloud. Then I gave a bag of candies to our friends' tearful, youngest daughter. During the long drive home, our new puppy slept on my lap.

From the very first night, Thundercloud groomed the puppy and comforted her. She had been a superb mother to two litters and knew just how to care for a tiny pup. I didn't know if she missed rambunctious Russell, but she seemed ecstatic to nurture our dainty new daughter.

Buster loved wrestling with his golden-eyed little

girlfriend. Even though he weighed sixty pounds and she was smaller than Wrex, he let her scramble up to the top of his neck and "win." In a few days, our frisky ball of farm fluff had become our amazing little princess. We decided to name her Gracie.

As Buster watched us nurture and love Gracie, he became calmer. He was no longer head shy. He didn't shrink away when we were angry. He didn't snap if we touched his tail. Perhaps watching us care for Gracie was healing his memories of an abusive puppyhood. We had earned his complete trust.

We left Gracie in the care of Buster and Thundercloud while we pushed the politics forward. The November election was imminent and every candidate had a close race, including the president. I chaired two fundraisers, one featuring the president, the other featuring the vice president's wife. I also went on countless road trips with Earl. By then, he was chartering a single engine plane to get him around our vast state. One Saturday, I wanted to bring Buster.

"No problem," said the pilot. "My wife and I fly with our dogs all the time." So, Buster trotted right up the plane's little staircase. During take-off, I held him against my chest while he looked out the window. He trembled with excitement when we taxied, then he rose up and stared down at the ground while we became airborne. He squealed a little, then yawned, and continued to watch the sky. I had no idea this was the first of many plane trips we were going to take together.

When we landed, he trotted out of the plane and was greeted by over-worked campaign volunteers. They were delighted we had brought him; the sight of a pet seemed

to help them feel human again. And I knew Buster was delighted to be around people hard at work.

To keep Buster even more amused, I started taking him with me more often. On a snowy winter day, a hardware store customer said to me, "I know that dog. We see him all the time at our friends' house."

"He's my dog."

"Oh, we thought he was theirs. He's such a wonderful dog. I wish he was ours."

Because I had seen so many people drawn to Buster, I began to be afraid someone might steal him. *What if someone puts him in a locked pen? What if they take him so far away, he can't find his way home?*

Then, one spring night, Buster and Gracie were both gone. I phoned several neighbors; they hadn't seen them. Earl and I drove through the neighborhood, calling to them. No pups. All we could do was wait. And worry. When we checked our answering machine, there was a message every pet owner dreads.

4

Needing to Negotiate

"I have your dogs," the male voice on our answering machine said.

I clutched a clump of Thundercloud's shaggy fur, and listened.

I was paralyzed with fear. Dognapping was a business in affluent Santa Fe. Friends of mine had paid thousands of dollars to get their dogs back. One had asked the police to watch the payoff and the return of his pet. The police arrested the thief, but didn't jail him. The dog was gone a week later, and never returned. And some people were wicked to animals. Every month, there was a news story about a dog being poisoned in Albuquerque, even dogs in fenced yards. *I'll never see them again!*

"I've fed them, and they aren't hurt," the message continued.

Earl returned the call. I was too frightened to speak.

The man had seen Gracie and Buster on the shoulder of the road, right in front of our house. Assuming they were lost, he invited them into his car. They hopped right in, and he drove them to his home. When Earl went to claim them, the man refused a reward.

Since this could happen again, we decided we had to improve our fencing. The barbed wire fence surrounding our property wasn't keeping our dogs at home. Fortunately, when Buster and Gracie were "taken," electric dog fence systems had just become available. We rushed to have one installed.

The system always kept her at home, but not him. Gracie didn't dare cross the shock wire. But on the rare occasions it lost power, Buster knew it. There was no warning beep, no mild shock, and no staying home that day. Scolding him was pointless. Keeping him caged in our small dog run would have been cruel. Negotiation was the only option, and he was quite a negotiator.

He had already made several deals with us. When he was on our bed he wanted constant petting. If we stopped petting him, he growled. When he turned around, ready to sleep, with his head facing the foot of the bed, we were not to touch him or move. Same growl. On Saturday walks in town, he wanted to be on the long, retractable leash. A regular leash made our pace seem too slow, so he tugged at it constantly. If I entered a building and left him tied outside, he howled. He preferred to stay in the car, even with the windows wide open. When we drove through McDonald's, he refused to eat their chicken nuggets. Burger King's were acceptable.

To make up for imposing the electric fence on him, I agreed to take him everywhere, even to the office with me. Beginning then, he wasn't just my dog; he was my constant companion. To me, he became a person. This extraordinary relationship was about to change my life.

5

Falling in Love

I took Buster to the law firm every day. While I sat at my desk, he stationed himself in the doorway to my office, always facing the building's entrance. He lay on the floor with his front paws crossed, and watched everyone work. When clients arrived, he stood up and greeted them with a smile and a wagging tail. We were the only business in town with a tuxedo-clad maitre d'. A few times a day, he opened the screen door so he could go out and patrol the garden, always coming back without being called. One day he came streaking into my office, then lay down under the desk. In a few moments, our office manager knocked on my open door.

"There's a policeman outside," he said. "I think he's here about Buster."

"Is he angry?"

"Really, really angry."

"Ask him to talk to Buster's lawyer."

The officer was fuming because our dog had slipped out of his grasp and outrun him. Earl assured him it would never happen again. Buster wore a county license tag because we don't live in the city limits. But our fugitive from justice was issued a citation for not wearing a city tag. The officer needed to save face.

Buster kept Earl's promise; he never wandered away from the office again. Instead, I took him on daily walks through town. His smile and dancing pace told me these promenades were his favorite activity. To reward my attentive behavior he almost never pulled on his leash. Without hesitation, he would lead me up steep flights of stairs, into elevators, or down the city's only escalator. We shopped in stores that welcomed both of us and avoided the few that didn't.

His company had a calming effect on my moods. Each busy day, I felt less edgy. If I became impatient with someone in a store, Buster would stand up and hug me as an effective reminder to be calm. I behaved better when I was with my dog.

Planning his nightlife was challenging. Earl and I didn't know how Buster might tolerate being left alone inside the law firm, so he would sleep in the car whenever we went out for a quick meal. When we went to a long evening meeting or reception, we would take him home first. Each time we drove away, he would stand in the driveway, looking heartbroken. His eyes seemed to ask us, "How could you? How could you leave me behind?" We grew to know that look well.

When Earl's chairmanship ended, our political schedules were less intense. As a couple, we continued to be an image of success: we had been married eighteen years, our son Cody had a job with an international folk art company, we were good business partners, our hotel business was growing, the law firm was doing well, and we had friends all over the country. But our focus on stress and thrill continued to extract its price: we no longer shared much affection or trust. At home, we were friendly, caring and distant. Each of us stuffed our feelings inside. We ate too much, drank too much, and thought we were getting along just fine.

I shared most of my love with Buster. I had been a lonely only child and his affection gave me comfort. His attentiveness and protection made me feel special. When we came home for an afternoon nap, cuddling was an indulgence for both of us.

I realized I was a little bit nuts, but he was the fellow who was "there" for me. He was my best friend, my lifeline.

I felt like a traitor when I made plans to go away. Buster would give me the "how could you" look before I brought out my suitcase. Sometimes, I made sure my husband could stay home with him. Whenever Earl and I traveled together, our office manager's mother would be our devoted house-sitter. She was in love with Buster too.

When I was home in Santa Fe, Buster and I did a lot of work together. He strolled around the meeting table when Earl, Cody and I were interviewed for, then granted, the

lease to start a small retail company. When we joined a pet outreach program, Buster charmed several old ladies in nursing homes. He lay at my feet during partnership and re-design meetings at our hotel in Santa Fe. While our company built a hotel in Albuquerque, I took him to meetings down there.

During late summer nights in Albuquerque, Buster stayed by my side, watching me work on furnishings. The first night we stayed alone in a guest room, he taught himself to sit by the door while I inserted the card key, then to stand up when the "click" meant the door could open. He entered the room first, to make sure it was safe for us.

6

Taking the Next Steps

I kept so busy I didn't notice Thundercloud becoming a dotty, arthritic old lady. She turned eleven in October, and spent most of her time asleep. Gracie seemed very bored; and I decided she needed a playmate. So, Buster, Earl and I went to the animal shelter and found Reggie, an eight-month old "mostly Border Collie." When Reggie met Buster, he lowered his head in deference. When we brought him home, he was sweet with the "girls" and didn't bother Wrex.

Long hikes in the forest helped Reggie bond into our little family. But when mountain snow covered the hiking trails, we needed another activity. To my delight, a friend with horses asked me to ride with her.

Thundercloud's arthritis prevented her from going on rides. So the other three dogs came with me. They played

well with my friends' Labradors, Cowboy and Sugar, and caught up with the horses when we cantered. During each ride, my dogs circled us, running up and down the hills to make sure we were safe. Cowboy and Sugar stayed close to the horses. Most horses are apprehensive about potential predators, but these seemed calmed by all that protection. The dogs did the worrying for them.

On the Saturday before Thanksgiving, we lost Thundercloud. She was lying very still, and wouldn't stand up, so I rushed her to the animal hospital. The doctor told me she died in the car. When I returned home, Earl and I held our other dogs, and sobbed. It was a sad day for all of us.

As I sat in a chair crying, Buster put his paws on my shoulders and hugged me. While I moaned for Thundercloud, I realized my boy was eight, and he could be the next to go. *We might only have three years left.* We weren't going to waste a minute.

So when Earl and I decided to spend a month in Quogue, Long Island, to see about building on some land we bought there, I wouldn't go without Buster. Gracie, Reggie and Wrex could stay with the sitter, but I wanted my Buster with me. In January, we signed a contract to rent a dog-friendly house there during June. I spent the next four months moving Earl's downsized law firm into a smaller building, flying around the country to meetings, and researching ways to take my dog on a commercial airplane. There were no good options.

When Earl and I were ready to board the Delta flight

for Long Island, I gave Buster one of the motion sickness tranquilizers our vet had given me. I stuck the pill into a ball of butter I had brought from home. Then we latched our boy into a big plastic crate, kissed him good-bye, and watched two baggage handlers take him away from us.

I was a wreck. I couldn't know how Buster was feeling. *What does he think I've done to him?* I wished I had taken a tranquilizer myself.

———

We all loved being in Quogue. Buster charmed everyone Earl and I met. He followed us when we rode bicycles, helped us explore our new property, and ushered us to the village market. But he howled like a banshee whenever we stepped outside the house and left him alone.

Once, we tried leaving him for half an hour. When we returned, we found two door screens shredded into ribbons.

"Oh, no," I shouted. "Buster!"

He lay down and rolled over onto his back. In this position, he always reminded us of a white alligator: from chin to tail, his chest and tummy fur was pure white. It was impossible to resist him when he gifted us with the "white alligator." We petted his belly, and apologized for leaving him alone.

If Earl and I went out to dinner, one of our young cousins would baby-sit for us. But she wasn't available the night we had Broadway theatre tickets.

Planning to go to the theatre left us with a dilemma. New York City was two hours away, and the play was four hours long. Leaving our furry dog in a locked car was too

dangerous; the weather was hot, and someone could steal him. Leaving him with a hired driver was too risky; Buster could easily slip away and try to find us. I decided that inviting a houseguest to sit with him was the best solution. On that morning, a dear friend arrived from Washington: Chief of Protocol of the United States of America.

The ambassador was delighted to be left alone for an evening. Having just returned from a diplomatic tour of the Far East with the president, she needed some rest.

When we returned home, Buster stood up and hugged me. But I noticed a slightly apologetic expression on his face.

"An hour after you and Earl drove away," the ambassador said. "I opened the door to the back yard. The instant I got it open a crack, Buster dashed out in search of you. I drove all over the neighborhood, calling him. Then I asked people, 'Have you seen a black and white collie?' Someone told me most lost dogs were lured by the cooking smells at the Inn at Quogue. Sure enough, he was there. As soon as he looked at me, he got in the car. Then he slept on the bed next to mine for the rest of the evening." She knew several heads of state who were a lot more trouble.

Because I didn't dare leave Buster alone again, I didn't ride in Earl's new boat. He had been on the rowing team at Yale, so buying a double scull soothed an adult-long lust. The canals of Quogue were ideal for rowing, and he was in college boy heaven. One evening, at cocktail time, he asked me to bring my drink and ride in his boat with him. Torn between loyalties, I decided to let Buster stay on our dock so he could see where we went.

As soon as I eased my middle-aged hips into the

skinny, wobbly boat, Buster jumped in with me. He lay at my feet, determined to stay there.

From then on, almost every evening, we all went on a tour of the Quogue canals. Buster sat in front of me. Earl rowed while I studied the design of the houses, waved back to people who smiled and waved at us, and felt Buster's body quiver when he pinned his eyes on distant ducks.

Chasing birds was his favorite game. When we went for walks on the beach, he raced after shore birds, his tail spinning like a helicopter blade. Then he would prance into the water, smiling with a look of total bliss. As my husband and I shared Buster's childlike enthusiasm, we felt ourselves becoming close again.

While we walked together holding hands, I thought about our plans to build a second home in Quogue. *If we drive here from Santa Fe, Gracie and Reggie can come too.* Our carefree dreams were becoming plans for a house, but I doubted Buster would live long enough to see it. He was almost nine. I consoled myself by remembering what the announcer at the county fair had said about Border Collies, "...they often live well past fifteen."

Before the flight home, I forgot to give Buster his tranquilizer. When we landed in Cincinnati to change planes, we disembarked onto the tarmac. After watching Buster's plastic crate come out of the back of the plane, I asked a baggage handler to bring it to us. That was against the airline's rules, and he couldn't let us walk over to see Buster.

"How is he?" I asked. "Is he all right?"

"He's trembling. Like this." The man quivered for me, eyes bulging wide.

I stuck two pills into a wad of butter and handed it to him. "Please. Feed him this."

The boarding gate for our next flight was inside the crowded airport. We stood in front of the windows and watched loads of baggage being fed into our waiting jet. I didn't see Buster's crate. *They've lost him!* Then, we saw a motorized dolly plop the crate onto the blistering hot tarmac under the wing of the huge jet. I could only imagine how frightened Buster must have been. I was sure he was terrified of the earsplitting noise, of being alone and of being away from me. I vowed I would never put either of us through that experience again.

Buster arrived in Albuquerque sound asleep, and he was still groggy when we arrived home. Gracie and Reggie were thrilled to see Earl and me, but they didn't seem to know who Buster was. They growled at him, then sniffed his entire body. It took several minutes for them to accept him again.

When my husband and I got into our bed, we cuddled with Wrex and all three dogs. As I drifted to sleep, I felt relieved we were all safe and at home. I looked forward to a summer filled with creative plans and hopeful promises. But I wasn't prepared for the trauma that lay ahead.

7

Too Much, Too Fast

I spent most of that summer designing the Quogue house. I was working with a Long Island architect who didn't own a computer, so I made most of the changes on my computer at home. I was also designing a natural looking swimming pool for our Santa Fe house. While I met with the landscape architect and her staff, my dogs played in circles around us.

Buster and I needed more things to do together. My friends with horses had moved to Connecticut, so I was looking for a horse of my own. First, I had to find a boarding stable that would let me bring my dogs.

A friend of mine had just been hired to manage the area's largest equestrian park. I took Buster with me to see it, and we were introduced to two horse trainers who also had their dogs with them. As always, Buster got along with

his new friends. After a few introductory sniffs, tails wagged. The trainers found me a gentle horse, as full of personality as Buster. The horse was three years old, didn't have a name yet, and I wanted to call him Scully. But, before making a commitment to buy him, I carefully read the facility's contract.

It said dogs had to be "under control" inside the barn. They were emphatically banned from the polo field. They were allowed on the short trail next to the facility's property and out on the adjacent, public Bureau of Land Management (BLM) trails. With those assurances, I signed the contracts, then bought a used English saddle. By early August, I had achieved my lifelong dream of owning a horse. At fifty, it wasn't too late to indulge the little girl inside me.

But the adult me was feeling more stressed. I didn't have an office in my husband's down-sized new law complex, so I no longer shared his clerical staff. For the first time in over twenty years, I was handling all my administrative details alone. Our hotel company had sold the Albuquerque hotel and its sister property in development, and we were designing an addition to Hotel Santa Fe. Our retail business was in its infancy. My board obligations for the Kennedy Center and the College of Santa Fe had grown. I was also responsible for the design and construction of the pool and the Quogue house.

Our finances were strained farther than we had imagined. So we couldn't afford to delegate my tasks. Earl was dealing with the legal and financing challenges attached to our projects while he was running his law firm and taking care of his clients' needs. All of these pressures caused us to bicker with one another. I was sure these quarrels would destroy our marriage if we didn't get some guidance. So,

with stiff reluctance, Earl consented to see a psychotherapist with me. I made an appointment, a month in advance.

Riding Scully relaxed me. His half Clydesdale genes made him extra tall and very mellow. Although he was young, he was at ease on the trails, went wherever I asked him to, and never shied. Buster trotted in front of us when we explored the BLM land, and seemed to love having another activity to do with me. If we encountered a grazing cow, he would crouch down and glare at her. Like an obedient sheep, she would amble out of our way.

On some days, I cantered Scully on the exercise track next to the polo field. Because my horse was so young and inexperienced, his trainer gave us weekly lessons in the indoor arena. I knew Scully needed more training, but I didn't think I needed those tedious lessons. I had been an avid weekend rider as a girl and had taught kids to ride at a summer camp in Vermont. I was experienced, I thought, a real horsewoman.

The first time I rode Scully with a friend, Gracie, Reggie and Buster came with us. They loved being out on the trails again, and they assumed their usual patrol duties. My friend was a novice rider, and her horse was new, so we took a BLM trail slowly. I had almost cancelled because I had been up all night working on the Quogue designs. Even though I felt exhausted, a quiet ride out in open land on a gorgeous day was bliss.

When we returned to the equestrian center's gate, a polo practice was in progress. The polo ponies were playfully charging at one another and darting about the field. To my knowledge, my young horse had never seen a polo practice.

Because Scully was tall, he was hard to mount from the ground. So my friend dismounted and opened the gate for us. After we rode through the gate I turned Scully toward it, as a courtesy, so her horse wouldn't start for home. I held Scully's rein with one finger, letting him extend his neck to eat grass, while my friend latched the gate and re-mounted. When we were ready to ride to the barn, I kicked Scully hard to get him to stop eating.

Then I worried about violating the "no dogs on the polo field" rule. To make sure my dogs stayed close to me, I headed far away from the field, by way of the exercise track. As soon as Scully stepped onto the track, he started cantering. *What fun!* Then he started galloping: a thrill for me, but very bad manners. Riding toward home should always be paced at a walk. I was afraid my friend might panic when her horse started galloping after mine. I had to stop Scully, no matter how much fun he was having.

My mind was on so many things I forgot I still held the rein with one finger. I pulled back on it, and commanded Scully to "whoa." But he kept galloping, following the track as it curved back toward the polo field. *Damn, he's heading around the track! The dogs will follow us near that polo practice! I'll break the rules!* "Whoa," I shouted again. Scully kept galloping. "Whoa!" I pulled the rein so hard that I leaned back too far and was unable to sit upright again. I lay on my horse's back while my legs gripped his pumping sides. I felt like I was riding on top of a high-speed train.

Those are the last moments I remember. Nobody saw me fall.

8

In Sickness and In Health

I felt someone squeeze my hand. Then I heard the voice of one of the horse trainers. "Can you hear me?"

When I opened my eyes, I was on the ground, looking up at his face and a lot of turquoise sky. Next, I heard the barn manager say, "An ambulance is on the way, your dogs are in my office, and Earl's coming to take them home." Then I drifted in and out of vague awareness. I knew I was being moved onto a stretcher, riding in an ambulance, arriving at the hospital and concerned about a dermatologist's appointment I was sure to miss.

Months later, people told me they were surprised I didn't remember the commotion while I lay on the ground. I didn't remember the several people who were tending to me. I didn't hear the center's owner scold the Samaritan who moved my face out of the dirt and dry manure. "Don't

you remember the polo player from Argentina who took off his shirt to shade you?" one woman recalled. "His body was gorgeous!" I also wasn't aware of what my dogs did after I fell: Buster lay on top of me, and Gracie and Reggie lay on either side of me. Their job was to protect me. They had no disire to be on a polo field.

I don't remember much about the eleven hours I spent in the emergency room. Earl says I was very polite to everyone, and I did make sure he cancelled my doctor's appointment. He phoned Cody, who left work to come and visit me. I don't remember seeing my son's face, just the touch of his hand and, "I love you, Mom." I was aware of a male nurse assuring me I was going to live, and that I would walk again. "You were very lucky." He told me I would "probably" ride again. "You've had major trauma," he added.

"You've had major trauma," was the first thing each doctor said when he met me. After several X-rays, an MRI and other tests, they told me what I had sustained: a concussion, two broken right pelvic bones, a broken right rib, a shattered left collarbone, a cracked neck vertebra and "major trauma."

After a week in the level just below intensive care, I was released from the hospital. I was wearing a sling and a plastic neck brace. With my good arm, I was leaning on a hemi-walker. I was only given follow-up appointments with a neurosurgeon and an orthopedist, as each person who released me said, "You've suffered major trauma."

I needed to stay in a hospital bed for a month. We rented one, and had it placed in the kitchen so I could watch the pool builders through the French doors. Getting out

of bed to feed myself, or use the bathroom, took forever. Buster walked next to me wherever I hobbled, careful never to bump against my painful right pelvis.

Despite my hurting body parts, I wanted to see Scully. After almost every fall in my life, I had been able to get back on the horse. In fact, I consider "get back on the horse" one of life's great lessons. It certainly kept me from being a quitter. Getting back on is essential for the rider's confidence and for the horse's discipline. I wanted to visit with Scully and tell him the fall wasn't his fault. He must have been doing everything he thought I wanted him to do.

On my first Saturday home, Earl drove me to the stable. We stopped at a Target store on the way. As I trudged through the busy store, wearing all my therapeutic contraptions, two little children pointed at me and screamed.

So when I approached Scully, I talked to him a lot. I didn't want the sight of me to frighten him, too. I assured him I loved him and he had done nothing wrong. Being with him and stroking his neck brought great relief to me. But nothing quieted my mind.

I couldn't stop reliving the accident, even when I was trying to sleep. I went over it again and again trying to decide what I had done wrong, how I lost my seat, how my body must have hit the ground, what I should have done differently. I relived the kick, the gallop, the decision to stop, the pulling back, the whoas, and the dozen wrong decisions. I was too tired to be riding; I should have cancelled the date with my friend; I didn't know to lunge my horse first; the reins were still oily from my cleaning them the day before; I was wearing gloves and didn't feel the reins' texture; I let Scully eat, giving him too much rein; I didn't know he

would be playful around other frolicking horses; I was too hung up on the polo rule; I was too worried about someone else; I was paying too much attention to my dogs; I didn't shorten the reins; I didn't grip hard enough with my legs; I should have let him canter around the track and stop on his own; I didn't think about my own safety; good thing I was wearing a helmet. I had made a lot of hasty, careless and ignorant choices. Bottom line: I was arrogant.

I thought about famous people who had been injured or killed because they made arrogant decisions. Death by arrogance: it almost killed me.

Even though the mental re-runs and the pain were constant, I avoided taking pain medication. Painkillers put my brain to sleep and made me depressed. I'm depressed enough, by nature. My body hurt everywhere, and my nerves were confused. When I was able to raise my leg and step into the bathtub, my right foot told me the water was scalding but my left foot said it was freezing. Touching a broken bone was agony, so I couldn't sleep on either side. When Buster put his paws up on my bed, I often asked him to come up and cuddle. He lay on top of me and rested his head against my chest, never touching a single broken bone.

After the first week, my rib stopped hurting. The collarbone and the pelvis would take more time. I had no energy to leave the house, wasn't allowed to drive, was still required to wear the neck brace, and needed the hemi-walker and the sling. I had no experience with injuries like these, but my doctors told me my bones should heal in six weeks.

Even though my body was on hiatus, I was deter-

mined not to delay the Quogue project. We needed to get the design locked down, and were almost at that point. The cost estimates were sure to go up if I let time pass. Soon I had enough energy to keep up with the slow pace of each design change, watch some TV news, and microwave a Lean Cuisine for myself. I did, however, cancel our appointment with the psychotherapist.

But I refused to cancel an appointment we had near Quogue. The construction meetings, approvals meetings, and building site visits were going to require a lot of trips there, and we needed a place to stay for a year while all of this was happening. Before my fall, I had used the phone and the Internet to rent a cottage in the next town. The cottage's owners insisted on meeting their prospective tenants, and I wanted to see the place before we signed a contract. This rental had been hard to find, and I was afraid someone else might get it. I could hobble to the bathroom and slog through Target, so I was confident I could get through an airport. There would be plenty of time to rest.

So, ten days after my fall, Earl and I went on the trip. I took my hemi-walker, my neck brace and my sling. I didn't ask the doctors if I could go; they were sure to say I shouldn't. My arrogance assured me I was protecting my broken bones. But I was too ignorant to protect my psyche.

I did well on the trip going there. People in airports gawked at my contraptions. But nobody screamed. The Delta representative in Cincinnati asked me what my needs were, and how they could assist me. To save my energy, I sat in a wheelchair and Earl pushed me down the long corridors.

The trip was worth taking. The cottage was tattered,

and a little depressing, but fine for a year of short visits. There was a dock for Earl's rowing scull, we had permission to re-arrange furniture, and we could bring Buster. I didn't know how I was going to get him there, but I wanted to be sure he was welcome.

We stayed at our cousins' house the two nights we were in Quogue. Their kitchen table was perfect for studying the plans with our architect. I slept on their downstairs sofa because I wasn't able to climb stairs without hurting my pelvis.

The flight home was difficult for me. Exhaustion made me irritable, but I also felt oddly disconnected from everyone, like a lost foreigner. I forced myself to hold my temper. *Just act like a sheep, part of the herd. You'll get home.*

The gate agent In Long Island insisted I board the plane last, rather than pre-board. So I managed the stairway from the tarmac to the plane in this manner: one sideways step up (*Ouch!*), rest, lift hemi-walker; next sideways step up (*Ouch!*), rest, lift hemi-walker. When I finally made it on board, a passenger tried to help me to my seat by pushing my hips for me. *Ouch, my broken pelvis!* I squealed in pain.

When we landed in Atlanta, we waited for the plane to empty, then made our way down the stairway. I saw the other passengers go up some stairs and into the terminal, but Earl I were ordered to enter a waiting van. When we approached the van, we were told to climb inside. I told the driver I couldn't make it up the two-foot high step from the ground to the van without a step stool. She stood next to me and spoke in a volume that implied I was deaf and retarded, not just a little immobile.

"We have a two hour wait," I told her. "So we'll go

into the terminal with everyone else and walk to our next gate. We'll be fine. Thank you."

"You can't do that. You're supposed to ride in the van."

"But I can't get in it. The step is too high. I can't move like that."

Without warning, she put her hands under my buttocks and shoved me into the van. The shock, and the shooting pain to my broken pelvis, caused me to scream my absolute loudest. When we arrived at the entrance to our gate, I had to climb out of the van. Two airline employees stood and watched me, then pointed at two flights of stairs leading to the gate area.

After Earl and I climbed the stairs very slowly, we sat in our boarding area. I didn't want to sit for very long, so I practiced walking to the rest room. I was determined to get this infirmity behind me. Needing help and being different were humiliating. I wanted it over with, wanted to be "normal" again. I thought about how awful travel must be for people with permanent physical disabilities. My close friend, Justin Dart, Jr., the driving force behind the Americans With Disabilities Act (ADA), had spent decades lobbying for people with disabilities. They simply want access to the world everyone else takes for granted.

After college, I had a close friend who, like Justin, was permanently disabled by polio and relied on a wheelchair. I had always felt sympathy for my friend, and thought I understood her apprehensions about going places and her need for ramps and elevators. During building design meetings for our hotels, whenever someone complained about the costs of putting in elevators, special fixtures and ramps

for "those people," I pointed out that each of us could be one of "them" at any time, with no warning. But until that plane trip home, I never knew what humiliation "they" endured daily.

After my second week of healing, I was able to use the computer. With my left arm still in its sling, I was able to type with both hands. Fortunately, my "mouse" hand was on the right. Buster stayed by my side when I was at my desk and greeted the pool workers when they knocked on the door to ask me a question.

Exhaustion prevented me from accomplishing much, and eating made me sleepy. So, I ate very little. When I had healed enough to drive, the neurosurgeon permitted me to have a thirty-day "handicapped" tag in my car. Doing errands would have been impossible without one; it took lots of energy to walk to and from my car, especially when I was carrying a package. Justin's words about the economics of the ADA became clearer to me: people with disabilities want to earn money and spend it. They don't want to waste their perfectly good minds and talents sitting alone in poverty, draining the economy while they depend on tax dollars. I had become one of them, and a defender of "handicapped" parking spaces forever.

My neck brace came off after week four, but the constant pain in my pelvis and shoulder continued. The orthopedist took more X-rays, and said the pelvis was healing well. I could stop using the hemi-walker. The collarbone was not healing, even though the sling had kept it immobilized.

"These clavicles have been known to never knit together," he said. "It's rare when that happens, and I've never seen one that didn't. We human beings don't really

need collarbones. They aren't actually what holds each arm in place. We'll keep looking at yours, and see. You can take the sling off in two weeks, then come back in five weeks. We'll take another X-ray." He told me clavicle surgery involves a large incision, a permanent scar, and a very long recovery period. It was too soon to decide if I needed that. I wanted him to tell me when I could ride again. *And when can Buster hug me again?* He couldn't say how long I would be feeling pain. Nor could he know I was going to suffer from more than a useless collarbone.

9

For Better and for Worse

The pool was finished in late November, and I was pleased with the results. I still had dozens of design decisions to make for the Quogue house, and I needed to prepare the rental cottage to be our base there. Still moving at the pace of a rusty robot, I boxed some old clothes and linens, then asked Earl to mail them to our address at the Quogue post office.

During the next plane trip to Long Island, I walked with caution. I kept a constant grip on Earl's upper arm to prevent people from bumping against my painful left shoulder. When we arrived in Quogue, we picked up our leased Ford Explorer, collected our boxes from the post office, and drove to the rental cottage. I decided I couldn't stand the place until we re-arranged the furniture, stored some of it in the attic, and bought some decorative items of our own.

Because of my aching pelvis and left shoulder, I could only lift with one arm and I continued to limp. I had very little energy and a lot of trouble sleeping. It took three days to get everything done.

Earl kept working, even though it was Thanksgiving week. His cell phone rang several times per hour, and he responded to e-mails on his laptop. I used the laptop to store the design plans for the house, and I could enter any changes.

When we finally had the cottage arranged to my liking, we were exhausted and felt we both deserved a rest. When we sat on our newly slip-covered loveseat, I poured each of us a glass of wine. We were finally settled into our cozy little nest. It was our first romantic moment since my accident, twelve weeks before. Earl carefully put his arm around me, and I nestled against his shoulder. Then his cell phone rang.

He answered it.

Now?

"No, not at all," he said to the intruder. "You haven't called at a bad time."

That moment marked the beginning of very bad times for our relationship.

It had been three months since the accident and I still couldn't bear to be touched on my left side. Turning my head hurt that shoulder. Lifting anything with that arm was intolerable. My pelvic area was still tender. Any unexpected touch was painful and frightening. Even a slight tap made me bristle and yelp. If I was going to be touched, I needed

to be warned. If anyone stood behind me, I jumped aside. Even though I dreaded being touched, I desperately needed to be held in someone's arms.

Earl said he understood what I was feeling. But in frequent absent-minded moments he touched me without warning, and I screamed in pain.

The week after Thanksgiving, we traveled from Quogue to Washington, D.C. During the trip, I kept reminding him not to touch my sore spots.

We got through the Kennedy Center Honors weekend, touching only when I gripped his upper arm for protection from other people. Sometimes Earl forgot about my condition and left me alone in a cluster of handshaking people, but we got through the trip home to Santa Fe without any major moments of humiliation or pain. As we entered our house, Buster greeted me with a whiney hello and a wagging tail; he even stood up to hug me. But he never put pressure on my left shoulder.

I began to worry about my speech; it was sounding a little slurred to me. Some words were hard to form in my mouth, and they came out muddled. So I scheduled some sessions with a brainwave therapist who had helped me overcome migraines. Because her office was in Beverly Hills, California, I had to travel again.

Earl and I made it through the trip to California and through the Santa Fe business parties during the Christmas season. But I never wanted to stay at a party very long. We were no longer a festive couple.

My constant fatigue allowed me to avoid any unnecessary communication or contact with my husband. In our bed, I put pillows between us to keep him from bumping

into my left side. Terse? Snippy? Sarcastic? I was all of those things, on a good day. I was building a house and recovering from "major trauma." Either of those things might make anyone feel like a monster. Stress on a marriage? Yes.

I was too tired to enjoy being with people, but I did enjoy the quiet company of Buster and Scully. Being around horses was very calming, even though my mind kept reliving every moment of the fall. *If that gate hadn't been next to the polo field. If I had only shortened my reins. I'm back too far! I can't sit up. How did I land?*

My orthopedist said I wasn't ready to ride, so Scully and I bonded in different ways. A few mornings a week, Buster trotted alongside me while I helped our trainer lead horses out to paddocks and back to their stalls. While I groomed Scully in the evenings, Buster lay in front of the cross ties and watched. The barn was open to anyone, and there were always new stall janitors. Having my boy there to protect me made me feel safe in the barn alone. Scully seemed to like his company too.

In mid-January, my horse trainer told me the owners of the equestrian center had announced that dogs were no longer allowed. She said a horse had been injured when someone's toy poodle ran behind him while he was being shod. She and the other trainer were still bringing their two dogs, because theirs were "grandfathered," permitted before the rule change. I had a contract and considered my dogs exempt from the new decision, also.

When I was given permission to ride again, I took a lesson in the indoor arena. Because my contract said dogs aren't allowed in the arena, I put Buster in the car. I thought he would be comfortable there. But as soon as I mounted

Scully, Buster started howling. He was so loud we could hear him from inside the arena. Clearly, he wanted to be with me.

Getting back on my horse was frightening, and Buster's constant howling made my tension worse. So my trainer tied Buster's leash to a jump in the middle of the arena. He could see me from there, and he stayed quiet. The next week, the arena was crowded with cantering hunter jumpers. Because Buster couldn't move freely, I was afraid he was going to be trampled. I looked at his wide eyes and knew he was frightened, too. From then on, he stayed in the car without howling.

My first time cantering again was terrifying. My big young horse was moving too fast, and my legs were weak from fear and lack of use. It took all the courage I had to keep my seat, because falling was not an option. After several lessons, I learned how to slow Scully down and stop him. But the fear of falling took all the fun out of riding. Any outside noise—a car's honk, a truck's engine, a bird's call, a tool dropping—made me flinch. When I flinched, Scully flinched, then shied. These abrupt, turning lurches terrified me. I had to learn not to react to my fears; I had to stay calm for both of us.

Aside from learning to ride all over again, and feeling comforted by Buster's unwavering attention to me, I have few clear memories of how I spent the next few months. I wasn't in a fog or anything like that; I was just very distracted. I remember feeling weighed down by fatigue, getting lost in familiar stores and forgetting which roads led to familiar places. I know I devoted my time to resting, finalizing the Quogue house plans, and overcoming my fear

of riding. But I have few memories of actually doing those things. My calendar for that winter is full of activities: trips to Quogue, trips to the brainwave therapist, and Earl I even started seeing the psychotherapist. I don't recall anything that happened during these events, but I'll never forget what occupied my mind: reliving that fall from Scully, over and over again.

I always relived it when I was driving to the stable. I could feel adrenaline start to rush through my system, a mile before the driveway. I held my breath every time I rode Scully at a trot or a canter. And I was always tense and irritated with people.

I also remember tremendous anxiety about money. The economics of the Quogue house were overwhelming. If we couldn't rent it for July and August (over a year away) we could not afford to keep it. Since most renters choose summer homes by mid-March, we had to have our house furnished by February. Once we signed the construction loan and the builder's contract, there was no turning back on this commitment. I was questioning the future of my marriage and had no use for an expensive second home. The house only made sense to me as an investment, if and when we sold it. I was starting to detest the entire folly and everyone involved.

This was especially true regarding Earl. I could no longer stand to be near him. By spring, we were seeing Dr. Joe, the psychotherapist, twice a week: once together, once separately. Buster always came with me.

I told Dr. Joe how I felt about Earl. "He's a caring, wonderful person. I've always felt lucky to be married to this man. I love him very much." I had no desire to find someone else,

but little things about Earl were starting to infuriate me.

"The big things in life don't often break up marriages," Dr. Joe said. "It's the little things that do."

One of our biggest little things continued to be my fear of being touched. My final X-ray showed that my collarbone was never going to heal. It still hurt, but the pain was not expected to last forever. Sleeping remained painful. I still bristled and snapped when Earl touched me, and often screamed in surprise when he entered a room. I worried about the Quogue house and didn't want to go out, even to dinner or a movie. I especially didn't want to do anything that involved other people. If we paid for tickets to a charity party, the cost became a tax deduction when we didn't go – another reason to stay home. I was tired and had no tolerance for noise. Getting the house built and furnished were my only goals. I wanted the project to end before it killed me.

On the monthly trips to Quogue, I missed Buster. I missed his calming influence. I was tolerant of people and noisy places when he was with me, but felt agitated when he wasn't. He was the companion I craved. My husband's companionship annoyed me, and I didn't know why. I felt guilty about those sentiments, but I didn't want to live with anyone. I didn't want to talk to anyone. I didn't want to eat anything except protein bars.

I lost thirty pounds that year, and felt no pride about that. It wasn't an effort. I no longer wanted to mingle with people in restaurants or grocery stores. I didn't have time to prepare food, and the clatter of dishes was irritating. Eating less food became a practical thing: weight and beauty had nothing to do with one another, but weight and energy did.

When I ate, I got tired. And I wanted to fit into one wardrobe, period. No more shopping for two different sizes and storing clothes that didn't fit. I had done that all my life. I no longer cared what I looked like, and I knew I was miserable to be with. I just wanted enough energy to get my house finished, to keep trying to ride my horse, and to be with my dog.

10

To Love and Protect

By early summer, I wanted Earl to move out of our house. I didn't trust him with any of the little things in life. He was a wonderful partner, but living with him felt intolerable to me. I was ashamed of myself for feeling that way, but I couldn't rationalize those reactions. They sprang from deep inside me, they were not thought out decisions. I became infuriated every time he forgot to do something, then denied forgetting it. I decided he was absentminded behind the wheel of a car, and I didn't feel safe when he drove. Certain he wasn't concentrating, I would scream in terror when a car slowed in front of us or approached our path from a side street. He was starting to snore at night, and sleeping was difficult enough for me.

I rarely went to Earl's office, and I seldom left the house, so I saw him only at home. My hackles rose whenever he ar-

rived, and those feelings seemed obvious to Buster. He slept outside the bedroom door when I took my early evening naps, but as soon as he heard Earl's car in the driveway, he jumped on the bed and lay on top of me.

Neither of us could afford a divorce. We were already under enough financial pressure. Each time I implored Earl to find another place to live for a while, he ignored me. I wanted my feelings to be taken seriously, and they seldom were. That was just part of our problem. Dr. Joe was helping us both shed childhood mind-sets. He also helped us realize that I had stored resentment from my days as a political wife. I had sacrificed my own emotions, needs and talents so everyone could admire Earl. We each had a lot of mending to do.

Buster had become my protector. He warned me when someone was coming to the door or when coyotes were howling outside. He also helped me in public. When I purchased something at a store, he stood behind me when I faced the counter. His slight tug on the leash told me he was greeting someone coming behind me. He was a lifesaver when I was riding.

When I was able to ride Scully on the short trail next to the equestrian center, Buster protected us both. In my teens, I had been a fearless cross-country bareback jumper, but I no longer had a thread of confidence. I was too frightened to ride alone, so my trainer rode next to me. Sensing my fear, my "mellow" horse shied at birds flying out of bushes. He was frightened when we came close to things he had never seen: large metal objects or blowing plastic trash. When he saw them, he would abruptly stop and refuse to budge, clearly wanting to race back to the barn. It was essential for

me not to let fear overcome me, and riding was teaching me to calm myself. I had to convince the horse to go forward, no matter how jumpy we both were.

Buster lifted our anxieties. He flushed birds out of bushes, far ahead of us, so they weren't a surprise to Scully. When Scully stalled in front of a peculiar object, Buster sniffed at it, wagged his tail, and smiled at Scully as if to say, "You big coward; it's only a pile of pipes." Then the horse would move forward. His sauntering gate seemed to reply, "Hey, dude, I knew that. I'm cool." I was sure they had the same conversation when Buster sat erect in front of a scary piece of blowing plastic.

Sometimes I sang to Scully when I felt him getting nervous. I sang to him to calm him down. My trainer said the singing actually calmed *me*. Once I was relaxed, my horse relaxed.

It never occurred to me to sing in airports. Even though they jangled my nerves, those crowded, noisy hornets' nests were obstacles on the path to Long Island. Each time we arrived in Quogue, Earl and I were thrilled to see our house going up. It was fun to stand on top of the wood frame and see our stunning views of the bay. We also loved becoming part of a delightful little village.

When we went to a community meeting in August, I noticed a woman with a dog standing in the back of the small auditorium. The dog wore a red guide dog jacket, but the woman didn't appear to be blind. I introduced myself to the woman, and asked her dog's name. "Lilly." Then I asked if I could pet Lilly. She gave me a reluctant look, then said something to Lilly that sounded like a gruff command to be off duty. As the woman watched me stroke the top of Lilly's

head, I asked her if she minded telling me why she needed the dog.

"Yes, I do mind," she said in an irritated voice.

I put my hands up in the "surrender" position and apologized. Then she told me what Lilly did for her. To protect the woman's medical privacy, I will only say that Lilly forewarned her about changes in her body. Before she became ill, the woman had been a powerful advertising executive.

When we returned home to Santa Fe, I wanted to find a way Buster could pass for a medical dog like Lilly. *Maybe he can ride in planes with me. No more being without him!* But my conscience scolded me for even thinking about undermining the hard-won ADA. I knew how many people depended on those laws for their freedom; they were Justin's people. Earl never even parked in a yellow zone, and he would surely not help me do something illegal. Dr. Joe told me only blind people were allowed to have these dogs. I told him about the woman I had met. He was sure Lilly was a rare exception.

A rare exception for me was a full night's sleep. The pain in my shoulder, the reliving of the fall, menopausal hot flashes, and worry about the building project continued to give me insomnia. At dawn each morning, I didn't wake up, I *gave* up. Earl and I decided a softer mattress might help—anything to improve my irritable moods.

We drove to the nearest furniture showroom. Buster came with us. The salesman welcomed Buster and ushered us to the bedding section. Then he asked us to lie on the pillow-top mattresses. Buster followed as we moved from mattress to mattress. All three of us lay on each of them for

a few minutes, trying to decide.

"Which one do you like best?" the salesman asked.

Buster jumped over to the first mattress we had tried. He plopped down and uttered a contented sigh.

We all laughed, then concluded it must be the best. So we bought it. For years, each time we went to that store, the salesman would tell us how much fun he had telling his colleagues about the dog who chose the most expensive mattress. Buster had become a legend.

I continued to avoid Earl as much as possible. I didn't want to keep hurting his feelings. When he traveled to a gathering of his college friends and their families, I decided to stay home. I had never missed one of his reunions before, but I needed time without him. On our twenty-first wedding anniversary weekend, he joined me on a Kennedy Center trip to Boston. Being too busy to focus on Earl was convenient for me; I didn't want to celebrate our crumbling marriage.

But we were still a charming social team and, by late November, we were starting to make friends in Quogue. It was an effort for me to be charming because I was in despair. Construction on our house had halted; two of the builder's other homes had to be finished by Christmas. I felt panicked. I was furious when I visited our job site and saw no workers, but there was nothing I could do. Yelling didn't help and it was too late to change contractors. I was so worn out I couldn't even cry.

I had time to relieve some pressure on weekends. Then I would bundle myself in fleece clothing and go for walks

on the beach. One blue-sky day, I saw the woman with the medical dog. I reintroduced myself to her, then to Lilly, and we walked together. I told her I missed Buster and wasn't the same person without him.

"Do you have any disabilities or illnesses?" she asked me.

She had shared her health information with me, so I told her, "Only mild clinical depression. And an unattached collarbone."

"You might be entitled to have a service dog," she said. "They can't ask you, you know."

"Who can't ask what?"

"It's illegal for someone to ask you to prove you have a disability. Not everyone knows that law, though. I travel with papers from my doctor, just in case I run into someone who doesn't know."

"Will they let you fly on airplanes with a guide dog?"

"Service dog, not guide dog."

"Sorry."

"Oh, airplanes have never been a problem. The airline people know the laws." She offered to lend me her file.

I returned to the cottage, ecstatic. I told Earl what the woman had said, but he was pessimistic. We borrowed the woman's file and, with her permission, copied some of it. She had letters from her doctor and from Lilly's trainer, copies of the ADA laws referring to service dogs, and a pamphlet from Delta Society National Service Dog Center, a resource organization for people who are assisted by service dogs.

The pamphlet paraphrased and noted the ADA provisions explaining that service dogs are not considered "pets."

At that time, they were allowed in all businesses open to the public *and* in any mode of public transportation. Also, it was against any person's right of privacy to ask for medical information.

Earl was wary about the idea of using the law to my advantage. But, driven by excitement, I was only sober about being punished for faking a disability. I had no idea, at that time, that I actually had one. When we returned home to Santa Fe, Earl researched the law. He found that the aid of a service animal was a medical option for people with disabilities, both physical and mental. Service animals were allowed on all commercial airlines. They could not sit in the aisle, in an exit row, or on a seat; the bulkhead area (if not an exit row) was to be provided if requested. At that time, there was no requirement to show proof the animal was a service animal, just verbal identification was enough. This was to protect people's privacy also. The animal had to be well behaved, on a leash, well groomed, and healthy. The owner was responsible for any damage to property caused by the animal.

I was delighted to learn all this, but my childish excitement was reined in by my adult conscience. I realized I could not violate this law and jeopardize people who needed its protection. I could walk (with a slight limp), I could see (better with bifocals), I could hear (when I wanted to), and I didn't have a chemical disorder (unless I drank too much). *Who am I kidding?* I felt ashamed of myself.

I read more of the law. In it, the definition of a disability was explained. A disability is an illness or condition, either mental or physical, which prevents a person from performing an essential function, such as walking, hearing,

driving or working. I participated in a lot of meetings for our businesses, but I didn't consider them "work" because my involvement didn't directly produce income. Going to these activities was my responsibility, but probably not what the law meant by "working." Functioning among other people all day had become impossible for me. I considered that to be sensitivity, not disability.

Then there was a list of mental illnesses that were considered disabilities. Depression was one of them. *I have that! I take prescribed meds for it!* But I could still function well in a work environment for a few hours, when I was feeling diplomatic and had the patience to focus.

Agoraphobia (fear of "the marketplace," or public gathering spaces) was another illness that got my attention. *I hate going out by myself, but that's because I don't like being around people anymore.* I wasn't afraid of anything out there, I just preferred doing my work from my house. Except for necessary meetings and a few small dinners, I hadn't been to anything social in a year. Then I read about Post-Traumatic Stress Disorder (PTSD).

I learned that PTSD usually sets in several months after a person suffers an injury or other form of physical or mental trauma. The early symptoms are irritability, tension, sleeplessness, weight loss, and an aversion to being touched. *Wow, I have this!*

I was stunned. Maybe my bad moods were because of a disease other than depression. Was I tense because of a disease, or because I was just under too much stress? Aversion to being touched? *I broke five bones; who wouldn't feel that way?* I wasn't ready to admit I had an illness. I still considered myself a busy person who deserved a few crabby

moments. Looking back on this stunned moment, I'm certain that if I had not read through those documents, because I wanted Buster near me, I might never have known I had a curable illness.

What can a service dog do for PTSD, I wondered. I read on and learned that, instead of having a lot of specific tasks to perform, a service dog can help someone with a mental illness "feel better" when trying to function in public. This might seem silly, but feeling better is essential when thoughts and emotions are in constant turmoil. It can make the difference between behaving like a crazy person in public or behaving somewhat normally.

Still, I thought, if I have this disease it isn't serious enough to be considered a disability. *Maybe I'm tense because of my broken bones, not because I'm the hopeless, awful person I often think I am.*

The idea that I might have a legitimate disability helped my conscience, a little. *Maybe I wouldn't be faking.* I thrived on having Buster with me, but was I ill enough to need him all the time?

11

Alone Together, at Last

When I asked Dr. Joe if I might have PTSD, we didn't discuss it much. I had more obvious problems that needed an immediate fix. In my sessions with him, I was a barrel of anxiety and we couldn't blame it all on one adult accident. I insisted my vitriol was caused by stress and by my husband's forgetfulness. Dr. Joe assured me we were removing layers of armor I had built around a swarm of emotions. I had been building this protection for fifty years. Over time I would find the way to my own truth.

"Trust the Process" was this doctor's favorite expression. When he first started saying it to me, I didn't know he meant "Process" as in the Universe, the Higher Power, a euphemism for the forces that hold life in place. Fortunately, I thought he meant the "process" of how he worked, his

method of therapy. I no longer trusted the Universe, hadn't been speaking to it for years, and wasn't going to let some optimistic therapist tell me I should. So, my incorrect assumption kept me from rebelling against my doctor and his process.

His busiest time was during the year-end holidays. "Families and alcohol don't mix well," he said. I didn't drink much, but I didn't mix well with anyone. At the few holiday parties we attended, I cringed when anyone touched me, especially if they approached from behind. I yelped when somenone grasped my tender left shoulder. *Why do you have to show camaraderie by gripping my shoulder?* If a woman bumped against me, she seemed to think nothing of it. *Ever hear of personal space?* I was not charming and was not jolly. I was worried about staying in a troubled marriage. I was worried about saving a stalled building project. "Humbug" to all.

So I turned to friends for part of a solution. Two families we know, with second homes in Santa Fe, travel on their own planes with their dogs. They fly from a private airport in Rye, near New York City. One family was planning to return east on January second; the other planned to fly back to Santa Fe in February. I boldly asked if they had room for Buster and me. I let them know I needed to spend a month in Quogue, so I could finish choosing furniture and "lean" on the builder. I was apprehensive about being alone that long, and would feel safer if Buster was with me. My unspoken and most pressing reason for going: to have some space from my husband.

Our friend flying east in January gave me an immediate "yes." Then he made room for us; he had one available

seat and some floor space for Buster. The friends returning in February weren't positive about their plans, but they welcomed us to join them if they came. As a precaution, I assembled Buster's crate, ducked an avalanche of guilt, and made a reservation for us to return on Delta Airlines. It was a gamble, but I had to get away.

During the five-hour flight to Rye, Buster was a perfect gentleman. He lay in his designated spot and stood up when people needed to walk past him. A few hours into the trip, the owner invited him forward to visit his dog, Tex. Buster and Tex, a champion Viszla, were frequent, rowdy playmates. On the plane, they wagged their tails, sniffed, barked a little, then returned to their "seats." When we approached the airport for our landing, I held Buster close to me. He trembled a little, but I could tell he knew what was happening.

On our first night in the cottage, we had no heat, so we cuddled together to keep warm. My left shoulder no longer hurt, unless I put weight on it, so we cuddled facing to the right. At dawn, we walked to the little beach at the end of the road.

The eerie morning light revealed no colors. I saw our little world in black and white. When Buster approached the snow-covered beach ahead of us, I heard wings flapping. Then I saw two swans flutter away and splash into the freezing gray ocean. I watched Buster run after them, black dog on white crust, until he skidded on the ice. Then he just stood and stared at them. They were the biggest birds he had ever seen.

I loved living alone with him. Whenever we were indoors, he stayed by my side or lay guarding the front door.

A thick layer of ice blanketed the neighborhood, and it was dangerous for me to walk him on a leash. So I opened the door and let him go out on his own. He always came back within five minutes. We were on a cul-de-sac and he couldn't go very far, but I didn't want to anger the neighbors.

One afternoon Buster made friends with the elderly couple next door. I introduced myself to them, and told them Buster was keeping me company for a month. They invited us for coffee and canolis, and were impressed by what a gentleman Buster was. After that meeting, they seemed to have given "the word" to all the other neighbors. Buster's forays onto their properties never raised one complaint.

While we were there, we had a lot of work to do. I shopped for furniture, and moved each piece into a storage unit. Twice a day, we went to the building site. Buster loved being around all those people working at their jobs. The builders would greet him with a "Hey, Busta!" and they considered him one of the guys. When they played with him, he would give them the "she never feeds me" look: his eyes opened wide, he would prick one ear, cock his head to the side, and wriggle a little. Those hard-working men gave him pieces of their brown bag sandwiches, every time.

During our free time on weekends, we visited friends. A dear couple in Quogue invited us both to dinner on Friday nights. They knew Buster was special, and welcomed him into their home as family. So he could enjoy the company of other dogs, I made some play dates with Lilly and two Labrador Retrievers we met on the beach. Bundled in layers of nylon fleece, we "moms" sat and talked while our "kids" raced around in the sand.

We took a long car and ferry trip to Connecticut and

visited our riding friends from Santa Fe. Cowboy and Sugar nearly burst with excitement when they saw their old friend Buster. They ran from the front door to the car, squealing in gleeful recognition. Then they all chased one another around the property, rolling in the snow. The horses whinnied and snorted when they saw me, and our friends welcomed Buster as their first "doggie houseguest." He slept in the guest room with me, and was very diplomatic when his friends wanted part of his breakfast. He didn't growl at them, he just barked once and glared; they both stood back. After a full morning of romping and running, Cowboy and Sugar were very sad to see Buster leave. He seemed tired, but happy to be going someplace with me. Long Island Sound was rough that morning, but he slept through the entire ferry voyage.

When we returned to our cottage, I checked my e-mail and read a disappointing message. Our friends had cancelled their trip to Santa Fe. We couldn't fly home on their plane. Even though I had reserved space for us on Delta, I dreaded making Buster fly in his crate. I actually thought about driving him home, across America in February. *Anything but leaving him alone in that crate!*

I shared my worry with my friend who had the service dog. As we watched Lilly and Buster scamper after one another along the hard, sandy beach, she insisted I go to private dog training classes. Lilly's trainer wasn't far away.

"But I don't really have a disability," I said. "And I'm don't want to abuse the laws that protect *you*."

"Do you still relive that accident?"

"All the time."

"Maybe you don't think you have a problem right

now. Suppose you get worse? Buster will know how to help you."

"But he's ten and a half years old."

"So?"

I watched Buster race after some seagulls, his tail high in the air. He pranced toward the water, chasing the birds into the waves. He spun around to look at my face, letting me know how happy he was. Then prejudiced thoughts began to poison my mind.

I'm perfectly normal, I protested to myself. *I'm not a sick person. I don't have a disability. I don't want to go around with a "service" dog all the time. I don't want to be labeled. I don't want people to pity me and treat me like an inferior. Earl and I will never be invited anywhere again. Earl will be embarrassed. Business at the law firm will suffer. We'll never be able to join the golf club in Quogue.*

But I did take Buster to meet a dog trainer. After telling him I felt awkward about going places with a service dog, I asked him, "What will people say?"

"To hell with what people say," he explained. "Don't get into a debate with them. By law, you and your service dog are required to be accommodated in any business open to the public, period. Nobody is 'letting' you bring your dog." That was part of our first day's lesson.

12

From This Day Forward

By instinct, Buster was already protecting me from unexpected touch. The dog trainer took us to a few stores and watched him shield my tender right leg by walking very close to my body. He watched Buster stand behind me when I waited at a counter, wary of other shoppers who were bustling behind my back. He watched Buster "greet" people before they came near me. Buster didn't just tug at the leash, he wagged his tail and got the shoppers to talk to him so I knew they were there. The trainer watched the way Buster would go through doors ahead of me to make sure our path was safe. Then he told me, "You're the dog who needs training, not Buster."

He showed me a video, starring several other dogs he had trained. I was amazed at what some of the dogs could do. There was a Lab who barked his owner into a corner

when he sensed he was going to have a seizure. A German Shepherd picked out items in a grocery store and brought them to his quadriplegic owner. Another Lab pushed elevator buttons; a chocolate Border Collie heard things then alerted her hearing impaired owner; and, of course, many dogs guided the blind. My needs were simple; I was fortunate.

"Not everyone chooses to benefit from the assistance of a service dog," the trainer reminded me. "For example, Stevie Wonder and Ray Charles don't use dogs. But they have lots of people helping them."

We spent an entire session practicing leash-holding techniques. To free my "lead hand" for other tasks, I tied knots in Buster's leash so I could hold it, at varying lengths, between two fingers. He hadn't pulled on the leash since my injury, so holding the end loop with one finger was enough contact. When we were dining, I put the loop around a leg of my chair. When I needed both hands to look through my purse, sign a credit card slip, or comb my hair in a restroom, I stood on the end of the leash. When Buster wrapped his leash around me, instead of using both hands to free him I lifted the leash over my head and pivoted around in a circle. When his leg got caught in the leash and my hands were full, I asked him to stand still. Then I put my foot on his leash and asked him to lift his paw. When I pushed a grocery cart, I held the leash in one hand and Buster walked next to the cart. He stayed right there next to me every time I changed direction. The leash made him part of my personal space, and I felt irritated when people approached him.

"It isn't proper to touch a service dog without asking," the trainer reminded me. "Even though Buster smiles at

people he isn't inviting them nearer. He's just putting them at ease, and telling you they're coming."

The trainer taught me what to say to people who tried to pet Buster: "Please don't pet him. I know he's adorable, but I need him to pay attention to me." Or, "Please don't pet him. He's working for me right now."

I needed to learn how to answer insensitive questions. Whenever a stranger approached me, especially one moving quickly, I felt nervous and became tongue-tied. The trainer told me that the questions people usually ask are: "What do you call that kind of dog?" or "What does he do for you?" The answers he recommended were: "He's a Border Collie," and "I have a disability; he helps me lead a normal life." The last reply was also a polite response to any form of, "What's wrong with you?"

The trainer gave me some Delta Society pamphlets to present to people, "if you want to educate them nicely, and get them moving on."

I thanked him.

Then he said, "If people make you feel nervous, just let Buster lead. He'll keep you moving forward."

He also taught me some diplomatic tactics: "If some employee questions your right to access a business, let him know you have a disability first, then tell him Buster's your service dog." He said it's best to call a restaurant in advance when bringing a service dog, and let them know the dog's size. "In Europe, dogs are welcome in restaurants, but not here. Some people are grossed out by the sight of animals around food. But that's their stuff, not yours."

He told me that restaurant managers are usually familiar with the ADA, can alert their staff, and will set aside

a suitable table for a patron with a service dog. Then he added, "Some pet owners see a service animal in a restaurant or other business place and expect 'Fluffy' to be allowed there also. So, even though a service dog isn't required to wear an i.d. jacket, it is courteous to use one in a 'no pets' establishment."

"What if someone doesn't know the law?" I asked.

"When an employee barring your entry is ignorant about your rights, don't try to educate that person," the trainer explained. "Ask for the supervisor, immediately."

"Okay."

"When you're in a hurry and an employee doesn't know what the term 'service dog' means, try saying 'medical dog,' 'disability dog' or the always reliable, 'I have a disability and he helps me lead a normal life."

"Good idea."

"Above all, protect your rights by protecting the law. Some big business owners are trying to find excuses to have the ADA laws repealed, all the time."

I opted not to have Buster trained to urinate and defecate on command. Most dogs can "hold it" for ten hours or more, and I didn't think finding places for him to go would ever be difficult for us. Besides, that additional training meant leaving Buster with the trainer for a week. Even if Buster *would* stay with the trainer, we both doubted he would learn this trick at his senior age.

But it is a very practical skill. When working in large urban buildings, such as airports or dog show arenas, there isn't always time to take a dog out to find shrubs and grass. One can lead a dog to a parking lot, an atrium or a tarmac. But unless he smells a spot that's been "tagged" by other

dogs, he may not know it's a place to pee. Without this training, how does the owner show a dog what to do? At best, an owner could mimic a dog peeing and hope the pet "gets it."

The trainer "graduated" us, gave us an i.d. card with Buster's photo on it and a red 'service dog' jacket. He also gave me a patch to sew on the jacket. It read, "Please don't pet me. I'm working." He handed Buster a cookie, and commented on how youthful and fit he was. Buster gave him a handshake and a smile, then looked to me for permission to eat the cookie.

It wasn't the trainer's job to decide if my illness was a true disability; that was my decision to make. I didn't consider myself ill. But Buster was ready to help me if I needed him. I knew he could do the work.

On the last day of January, I received a wonderful e-mail. Our friends' trip to Santa Fe was back on, and Buster and I were invited to fly with them. I clicked on the reply button and accepted.

I was sad to see our time alone together end. Buster was ten and a half, and our two adult sheepdogs had died at eleven. After all his help with the new house, I feared he was unlikely to spend any time there. *Everything in it will remind me of him.* Any thought of losing him made me cry. *But remember, "…they often live well past fifteen."*

I was aware that I depended on Buster to help me feel worthwhile. He saw into my heart better than anyone did, even my family and oldest friends. I told myself that if this smart, intuitive friend knows me and loves me, I must be

lovable. Maybe some people really do love me, and I should start believing them.

Knowing I felt sad, Buster nudged my hand, wanting to be hugged. I held him close to me and tried to stop crying. "You are the love of my life," I whispered. I wanted to live with him forever; I wanted time to stop. I realized I loved him more than anyone. Even more than my husband, to whom we would soon return.

On the day we left from Rye, Buster flew like a veteran. He trotted onto the little plane and nodded a polite hello to Heather, a Scottie who never left my friend's lap. Then he curled up on the couch and slept through the entire flight. When the plane came to a final stop, he was the first one at the door. He wanted to exit first, to make sure I was safe.

Earl met us at the airport. A month with Buster had softened me. I was happy to see the loving man I had married, and his gentle hugs let me know I was safe and at home. When we got in the car, Gracie and Reggie were waiting. As soon as they saw us, they wriggled and whined with excitement. When we entered our house, Wrex darted toward us to say hello. Buster sniffed each room to see what had changed, then he pranced outside through the dog flap. Gracie and Reggie followed him. They all trotted out to the lawn, then raced around in circles, barking.

While we watched our "children" at play, I held Earl's hand. When we went to bed that night, I had no desire to put pillows between us.

13

In Joy, Sorrow and Denial

While Buster and I were away, the owners of the riding stable hired a new manager, and Scully's trainer told me her new boss was determined to enforce the dog policy. Since there were no new written rules, and she was still allowed to bring her dog, I felt confident about my right to have Buster with me.

I had found enough courage to ride alone on the trail next to the stable's property, and was just beginning to ride out on the BLM trails with the trainer. I was too frightened to canter outside of the arena, and Buster's calming company was essential on the trails. I was still afraid to be alone in the barn, and needed him with me for protection. So whenever the new manager walked past our stall area, I checked to see that Buster was leashed, made myself very busy, and ignored him.

I continued to relive the accident, but I didn't realize my PTSD had worsened. I wasn't aware of the symptoms, because my stress about the Quogue house had eclipsed other concerns. At the end of my first week home, Earl and I attended a weekend seminar we participated in annually. I planned to meet him at the opening cocktail party; we didn't arrive together. I felt irritated when he wasn't waiting for me at the reception table and I had to search for him in the crowded hotel ballroom. When I got to him, I held his arm and listened to him continue his conversation with another participant. I felt tired and harried, so I whispered to him that I wanted to leave. He continued his conversation as though I had said nothing. So I left the room as fast as I could, claimed my car from valet parking, and drove home. Coming home to the loving attentiveness of Buster, Gracie, Wrex and Reggie was heaven. In our next session with the Dr. Joe, we discussed this "episode." I concluded that my anger was about feeling abandoned. It never occurred to me I really did have PTSD and felt panicked in a crowd of people.

I constantly felt agitated. I was sure my anxiety was about the Quogue house. In late February, Earl and I took another trip there to keep things moving forward.

I could no longer speak to the builder without becoming enraged. Because the construction wasn't finished, we had lost potential tenants. People loved the views of the bay, but weren't willing to commit to a house that was "expected" to be ready for summer. Our last chance to rent the house was the spring break visitors' season, and we needed to have furniture in place. I still had to order rugs for each room and blinds for all the windows. The cabinets needed to

be installed, and the swimming pool needed to be built. Earl was in charge of ordering the stereo system, the phones, the cable TV service and the alarm system. Also, the owners of the cottage wanted us out by April first, so they could rent to someone else for the summer.

My emotions were a mess. I had become an angry monster, and Earl and I showed no affection for one another. We rented a truck and collected our remaining cartons of furniture. Then we crammed them into our storage unit, bickering the entire time.

I phoned Dr. Joe. He reminded me that I was under an unusual amount of stress. He encouraged me to comfort the "little kid" inside me. Then he asked, "Do you miss having Buster there to take care of you?"

"I can't stand being without him."

Because I still had so much to do, I couldn't fly home with Earl. So I stayed a few days longer and lived with my aggravations, all by myself.

I missed Buster's company. I needed him to help me cope. I missed his prancing enthusiasm, his happy smiles and cuddly affection. The next-door neighbors missed him. The guys at the building site missed him. When I was in the storage unit one day, Jack, another renter's standard poodle, came scampering to my open door, tail wagging, hoping to play with Buster. I cried when I saw the crestfallen look on his curly brown face. I missed Buster so much, I ached.

I told myself my only hope to become normal again was to survive the completion of the house. Each day, I reminded myself that the end was closer than it had ever been before.

During a brief trip home to Santa Fe, Earl and I went

to the ballet. While I was standing near the will-call area, a man in a business suit grasped my shoulders from behind and edged me aside so he could talk to the ladies behind the reception table. I let out a startled squeal, and he apologized. My pelvis and rib had been healed for over a year, and the pain in my shoulder had been gone for months. This man's innocent gesture didn't hurt my body at all. Instead, it left me too shaken to talk, or to walk without trembling. Earl had to lead me to our seats after everyone else had settled into the auditorium.

On April Fools' Day, Earl and I moved our things into the Quogue house. We hauled all of the furniture out of the storage unit, carried each piece to its planned location, and put the cottage's furniture back in place. We did all of this in a pounding rainstorm.

After the move, I still had a lot of details to finish, but we needed to go home for a while. Earl was hosting a gathering of his college classmates who were coming to Santa Fe from all parts of the country. I had been planning to be with them, but was too stressed and exhausted to attend any of it. I preferred, as always, to stay home and cuddle with my darling Buster.

"When you're not here, he's so sad," our house-sitter told me. "Gracie and Reggie are fine. But I can tell Buster really misses you. He just isn't himself." I assured her I felt the same way without him. "That's why he's with me so much. I treasure every minute we have together."

Buster came with me to see my psychiatrist. He lay facing the door while the doctor and I talked. Dr. Joe had suggested I consult the psychiatrist about changing my anti-depressant prescription. Because most of the pressures

of the house were behind me, it was an appropriate time to discuss this. My stress level had returned to normal, and I could determine if a change in medications made a difference. The drug I was taking numbed my feelings of gloom, but it also numbed any feelings of joy. So I didn't want to take a larger dose. But since my self-image and erotic desires were both at zero, a change of medication was worth the try.

My psychiatrist told me there was a new generation of drugs with fewer effects on the libido. To update him on the events of my life since I had last seen him, I told him about the horse accident, the building projects and the severe emotional swings in my marriage. I asked him if, besides depression, I might also have symptoms of PTSD. He asked if I held my breath when I got nervous in public. "I do. My limbs felt weak too." I told him I felt disoriented in big stores and tried to stay near the walls. He asked if I continued to relive the accident, and I told him I was sure I always would. He said those were all PTSD symptoms, but as long as I was still functioning in a manner acceptable to me, I shouldn't worry about them.

"I'm not worried," I told him. "I'm sure it was just stress. Now that life's almost back to normal, I can start to be myself again—just a little neurotic, not totally frantic."

I shared what I had learned about people with mental disabilities and service dogs, plus how deeply comforted I was by Buster. The doctor was intrigued to learn more about service dogs and asked me to send him copies of my research. Dr. Joe asked for the information also. They both encouraged me to do something very special for myself, now that the Quogue house was built. Having survived a

year and a half of all that stress, I agreed that I deserved a reward.

I had never rewarded myself with anything but ice cream or dark chocolate, but I was sent a brochure that almost stopped my heart. It was an invitation for a three-week trip to explore the ruins of Petra, trek in Nepal, sight-see in China, visit the temples of Tibet and Burma, climb the ruins at Angkor Wat, see the famous horses of Mongolia and experience the culture of Uzbekistan—dreams I had held for decades. The trip was scheduled for November, months after the Quogue project would be behind me. I decided I had to go. If I had learned anything from breaking five bones, I knew my body wasn't going to be strong forever. I knew not to postpone my dreams. When I asked Earl if he would like to join me, he said, "We're too busy right now. Maybe some other time."

"That's why I've never been to any of these places," I told him. "I'm going."

The trip was expensive, but my father had left me some money to save for my final years, and life was growing shorter than ever. I had six months to study and prepare for the journey. My only concern was leaving Buster for a month. Knowing that Earl would be home with him made me feel a little better. I had overcome a lot, I told myself, and the stress was almost over. I deserved this reward. Buster would wait for me.

The house-sitter stayed with our pets while we went to Quogue to continue finishing the house. The landscaping wasn't finished, the pool wasn't finished, but Realtors were showing the house to prospective tenants.

After we returned to Santa Fe, we attended another banquet. We sat at a round table, and having my back to a lot of other tables made me feel nervous. I flinched when people touched me, so I sat in my seat sideways allowing me to see what was behind me. I didn't want to dance with Earl, because I didn't want to be bumped into. I didn't want to leave the table to say hello to other people. I just wanted to go home.

I was gaining more confidence on Scully, but his trainer told me the manager was getting serious about banning Buster. She could no longer intercede for me, because he didn't care about my previous agreement. My contract had been "lost." So I promised to keep Buster on a leash at all times. One day, when I mounted Scully to ride on the trail near the facility, the manager stood and watched me. He told me to attach Buster to a long lead rope and hold it while I rode. He said I could get off my horse and unhook the rope at the fence next to the trail.

Buster tried his best to stay away from Scully's huge, iron-shod hooves. I couldn't give Buster all the rope, because I was afraid Scully might trip on it. Buster twisted his body while he trotted next to us and pulled at the lead rope, begging for more distance. He looked terrified. My horse seemed afraid too. This was a dangerous and unnecessary humiliation for all three of us. So the manager, the trainer and I scheduled a meeting.

The manager was a genial, decent guy. I realized he was trying to do a good job, and I was making that difficult for him. When I arrived at the meeting, I brought Buster,

his jacket, some Delta Society pamphlets, and a copy of my contract. While the manager and I made some ice-breaking chitchat, he mentioned that his father was a retired judge. I revealed that I had helped campaign for his wise and honest father. Then I appealed to his sense of civic fairness, and stretched a thread of truth. I told him Buster was my service dog. "I have a disability, and he helps me lead a normal life."

I told him my disability was the result of a fall on the center's property, and I wanted to keep the symptoms to myself. The stables were open to the public for many events. The ADA required Buster to be leashed in public, but not to wear his jacket. So I proposed a deal: even though it compromised my privacy, Buster would wear his red "service dog" jacket. This would help the manager enforce the pet rule. I would continue to keep Buster leashed in the barn, but he could be off the leash when I was on (or leading) a horse. I said I could keep Buster close to us with verbal commands.

After that, whenever I was on Scully near the stable, I looked to see how close Buster was. If he was more than eight feet away from me, I called to him and said, "Stay close." That brought him right next to us. But when that manager entered the barn, Buster invented his own behavior.

I first noticed this when I was bent over, looking for something in my tack trunk. Suddenly, I felt Buster's paws on my back, as if he were trying to mount me. I turned to see what he was telling me, then saw the manager walking by. The next week, I was sitting on the trunk and putting on my boots. Buster raised up and put his paws on my shoulders. He kept his head turned toward the door, to show me

the manager was entering the barn. The third time, Buster stood up and put his paws on my chest, asking me to stay standing against a wall. The manager was leading a horse in our direction. Buster wasn't protecting me from the horse; he was protecting me from someone I wanted to avoid.

By the middle of June, the Quogue house was finished. I was proud of the results. All my planning had been worth the trouble; every detail was just as I had wanted it. The pool was an aqua marine jewel, the sod was laid, trees were planted, and each lamp, mirror, book, napkin and basket was in place, ready for the tenants we did not have. It was satisfying to sit by the pool with our favorite Realtor and raise a toast to our achievement. She just needed to deliver a tenant.

We returned home, excited about our creation. But we were afraid we couldn't afford to keep it. I actually asked the Universe for some help. *I know I haven't been speaking to you in a long time. But, please, bring us a tenant. Please.*

A week later, we got an offer for August. Since it was for only one month, the money was half of what we needed. But it was enough to keep us solvent, so we said, "Yes!" We were so ecstatic, we danced around the dining room with our dogs. Buster put his paws on my shoulders and bopped with me from side to side, Gracie chased her tail, and Reggie rolled over on his back and wriggled. I was feeling very good about life, and Buster was smiling with me. *Thank you, Universe.*

I could relax. The pressure was over, and I looked forward to having fun again. I dressed up for the opening

of the Santa Fe Chamber Music Festival and arrived at the Gala dinner on the arm of my handsome, smiling husband. We greeted people during the cocktail hour, then went into the dining room and found our table. As I had requested, my assigned chair had its back near a wall. While I was putting my handbag at my place, Earl walked away to talk to a friend. When I looked in his direction, I saw the friend speeding toward me, smiling. His arms were open wide in greeting.

My throat locked. My knees tightened. I couldn't breathe. My hands flew in front of me to protect my body and I stepped backwards, terrified. My mouth opened, but my throat felt paralyzed and I couldn't scream. Instead, I heard myself making high-pitched noises that sounded like "Huhgh. Huhgh." When I backed into a huge ficus tree planter, the man stopped walking. He looked at me with a shocked and bewildered expression.

"It's me," he said. Then he said his name. I heard the name and knew he was an old friend, but there was no recognition.

"I can't," I said. "Sorry. I can't." My mind and my mouth were not connecting. I couldn't form any more words.

Earl comforted our bewildered friend and explained that I was still recovering from a serious injury. When he returned to my side, I was trembling. I sat in my seat and continued to tremble. I don't remember the rest of the evening. I got through it, but I never wanted to go anywhere again. I felt embarrassed. I was afraid of how I might react in the future.

I was even afraid to go to Quogue. We had planned

another visit, to enjoy our house, relax with relatives, and make preparations for our tenants. But I didn't want to go. The image of being in a room with several people terrified me. *The airports. The grocery store. The cleaners.* I held my breath, just thinking about them. These environments, once so common, so essential, had become frightening to me. I knew it was time to admit I had Post-Traumatic Stress Disorder. It was time to admit it was interfering with my ability to live a normal life. It was time for a loving friend to lead me forward, back into that life. After all his years of looking, Buster finally had a real job.

14

Show Me The Way

O ur travel agent seemed skeptical about reserving space for a service dog. When I asked her to make our flight reservations, my e-mail told her, "I have a disability, and Buster has been trained to be my service dog." She said she had never booked a service dog before, just show dogs, so she checked with the airlines and learned that they all accommodate people with disabilities who use service dogs. She booked us on Southwest because they had the shortest connection between flights to Islip, Long Island. She explained the regulations about seating (Buster couldn't be on a seat or in an exit row), told me that I needed to bring a health certificate issued by a veterinarian within three days of each flight, and that Buster was required to wear his jacket. She told me we should check in at the ticket counter, not at the curb. I assured her I would comply, but

I was still afraid the airline wouldn't let Buster on the plane with me.

I took him to the vet to get his health certificate. "They won't poke you today," I assured him. He wasn't nervous at all. He seemed to know that being examined was a necessary part of his job. Not knowing what to do next, I phoned Southwest and asked them about their policy in the airport.

"Do I ask someone from security to escort me to the plane?"

"Not unless you would like us to provide someone."

"My service dog and I have never flown on an airline before. I'm very nervous. I want to be sure I know what to do."

"Ma'am, we do this every day. People with service dogs fly with us all the time. Just go straight to your boarding gate after checking your bags. You'll be fine."

On departure day, we drove to the airport with Buster and checked in, then we all went up the escalator toward security. As if it were any other doorway, Buster trotted through the metal detector ahead of me. The sensors didn't beep. Still holding his leash, I followed him through. No beeps for me, either. I kept him on a short leash as he guided me to the boarding gate.

Even with Buster next to me, I felt terrified of the all the people bustling around us. Many were pulling bags, and the wheels made loud ka-klaking noises as they jittered along the brick floors. Several parents were sheparding gleeful, scampering children. I was afraid one of these giddy little sprites was going to dart into my path and trip me.

A toddler shrieked, then pointed at us. "Look at the

doggie!" But Buster stayed focused on where he was taking me, keeping a steady pace by my side.

When we reached our gate, we waited in the pre-boarding area. There were no chairs that backed against a wall, so I sat on the floor and leaned against a window. Buster lay beside me, eyes alert, ears up, keeping watch. Earl went to the gate agents' podium and presented our drivers' licenses and Buster's i.d. card. I waved at the agent as she compared our faces to the photos.

My body trembled when anyone approached us. Earl noticed this and politely deterred people from coming over to pet Buster. People who needed a "puppy petting fix" were disappointed not to get one. Those who seemed afraid of dogs stayed far away. The pre-boarding agent told us he had cleared the front row for us; it was a bulkhead but not an exit. He asked us to board before any of the other pre-boarding passengers, and we took our seats. I sat by the window, Earl sat next to the aisle, and the middle seat was empty. Buster curled into a ball and lay under my feet.

"Would your dog like some water?" our flight attendant asked.

I had a red, collapsible canvas water bowl in my purse. When I put it on the floor for Buster, he wagged his tail and smiled at me.

"Yes. That would be nice," I replied. "Could I have some water also?"

"Sorry, Ma'am. I'm not allowed to give you anything until after take-off."

She brought me a can of water and watched me pour it into Buster's bowl.

"Would he like anything else? I have cheese crackers."

"He might like those. Thank you."

She brought him the crackers. He ate them right away.

Even though the plane was full, nobody sat between us. Earl and I fastened our seat belts and enjoyed the smooth take-off. Then we looked at one another with joyful amazement. Buster was flying to Quogue with us!

Buster stretched out and fell asleep, keeping his head facing the exit door. Just seeing him there made me feel calm. He slept through the entire flight. To give him enough room, I took off my shoes and propped my stockinged feet against the padded wall in front of us. During our twenty-minute stop in Chicago, a flight attendant offered to take Buster out onto the tarmac. When they returned, she told me he had been very eager to get back to me, and wouldn't pee. After more water and crackers, we arrived in Long Island.

I had breezed through the small Islip airport dozens of times, but that day I was almost paralyzed with apprehension that someone was going to bump into me. I had to convince myself to breathe and keep my legs moving. To protect myself, I kept my left side against any available wall while Buster buffered me on the right. Now a traveling professional, he smiled and kept his tail up while he trotted through the airport. Without Buster's calming influence, I believe I would have fainted.

In the baggage area we stood against a wall while Earl claimed our bag. Then we went outside and found some shrubs for Buster to pee against. He looked very relieved. After leaving the airport, we stopped to buy groceries, leaving Buster in the waiting taxi.

As soon as Earl and I entered the store, I could not let go of his arm. He had done most of the shopping since my accident, and I had forgotten how busy and noisy a supermarket can be. When another shopper darted past us, I threw my body against Earl's. I was afraid to walk down a main aisle. People whizzed by us, pushing big rickety carts, stopping suddenly, backing up, changing direction without warning. I was afraid to be left alone if Earl went to look for something. So we searched for each item together and avoided the main aisles. It took a long time to find everything, but there was no reason to function at our former, hurried pace.

Two days later, I drove to the town next to Quogue and took Buster with me. After I dropped some clothes at the cleaners, I realized I needed something at the supermarket. I was afraid to go in alone. So I put Buster's jacket on him, and let him lead the way. In the pickle aisle, a store employee approached me and said, "Ma'am, we can't let you have your dog in here."

I felt my knees weaken and my throat tighten. Remembering the banquet in Santa Fe, I was sure another embarrassing scene was imminent; again I would only be able to say "huhgh, huhgh" in response. I imagined Buster and me being thrown out into the parking lot, diet ice cream left melting in my shopping cart. I took a deep breath and was able to make my mouth say, "I have a disability and he's my service dog." *Exhale.*

"Oh, I'm so sorry, Ma'am," the man said. "Forgive me. I should have looked. I'm really sorry. We get people in here with all kinds of pets. You and your dog are more than welcome."

I was awed by how nice he was. Over the next several months, I was amazed to learn how nice people are. I had always been a little bit guarded out in "public," but now I had Buster beside me, in a bright red uniform, showing the world I was vulnerable and different. Most people were very kind. My faith in the goodness of people was being restored. But I did have a few insensitive encounters.

The first one was during that summer, at K-Mart in Riverhead, near Quogue, the other at Target in Santa Fe. Each time, the weather was hot but Buster was wearing his jacket. The bright red jacket that said "Service Dog" and "Please Don't Pet Me. I'm Working." He was strolling next to me on a very short lead, and an employee, from half way across the store, bellowed, "Hey, Lady! No dogs in here!" In each instance, I felt a naked lack of privacy and my body started trembling. I ignored the rude public shouting until I was approached directly.

"Ma'am, you'll have to leave the store. Your can't bring a dog in here." Instead of fear, I felt anger, then my anger turned to compassion. *This person hasn't been trained about the ADA, and may have just started this job.* Buster sat and looked up at my face; his gentle eyes assured me he was there for me. I pointed to his jacket and said, "I have a disability, and he's my service dog." The answer from each confronter was the same: "I'm sorry. I didn't notice."

Even though I was treated with kindness, I felt anxious in public places. Any approach made me tremble. If I considered going out, I still talked myself into staying home. In Santa Fe, I only wanted to go to the riding stable. If I needed to leave the house, I took Buster, I latched onto Earl's arm, or I didn't go. I didn't have the energy to be the

active organizer I had always been, but I still headed a committee for a women's networking forum. I arranged that work so I didn't have to leave home much. I communicated with people on the phone, through the mail, and by e-mail. I called meetings only when necessary, and made sure they were held in small rooms. If I went anywhere, I did the driving (both hands on the wheel, both eyes on the road), because anyone else's driving scared me.

During that year, Buster and I found a way of making conversation with one another. I was certain that three loud huffs meant he was saying, "I'm right here." However, when I panted to him, "Hhuff, hhuff, hhuff," he seemed to love it. Our "chats" often went like this.

Butster: "Hhuff, hhuff, hhuff."

Me: "Hhuff, hhuff, hhuff."

Buster, big smile, bright eyes, tail in the air: "Hhuff, hhuff, hhuff."

Me, big smile, big kissing sound, happy heart: "Hhuff, hhuff, hhuff."

We often huffed like this for several minutes. We loved it.

Dr. Joe encouraged me to get out into life, because staying at home so much wasn't healthy. So I accepted a few invitations, knowing Buster could come with me. He escorted me to a women's forum banquet in Albuquerque. He escorted me to my assigned table and lay next to me until the room filled. When waiters carrying huge trays of chicken Caesar salads started stumbling over him, he sat up and gave me a perturbed look. I snapped my fingers, and he looked at me for direction. I lifted the tablecloth for him and pointed. He lay under the table, with his head on my foot,

until the luncheon was over. I bent down and "hhuff'ed" to him a few times, and he "hhuff'ed" back. When the room was almost empty again, we left.

Throughout the luncheon, I saw many friends and associates. I sat sideways in my chair so I could stay alert to the movements behind me, but I yelped once when a woman put her hand on my shoulder. Starting on that day, I began to develop the skill of catching a person's hand before it landed on my vulnerable left side. When I saw a threatening hand coming toward me, I held it in both of my hands and said, "It's nice to see you." None of the women at the lunch asked me why I had a service dog. One friend made a quip about "bringing my doggie," then noticed his jacket. She looked at me and smiled with compassion, not pity.

When Earl took me to large events, an opera or a movie, I left Buster at home. "I don't want people stepping on you while you're asleep in a dark aisle," I explained to him. He would respond with a short squeal, then follow us to the car and stand in the driveway.

As we drove away without him, he would stare at me with an expression of astonished concern. His bewildered eyes not only seemed to be asking, "How could you?" They also told me that he thrived on doing his job, and that I needed him to take care of me. When we returned, he was waiting for us on the front pathway. When I got out of the car, he ran to me and hugged me. Then I pointed toward the house and told him, "Show me the way."

To avoid feeling trampled by crowds at cultural events, I would arrive early, stay in my seat during inter-mission, leave after everyone else, and never walk to the

ladies room. I'm sure I didn't seem like my "old" self to anyone, but I never enjoyed going out.

Large parties were intolerable. I didn't take Buster to those either. Private homes are not subject to the ADA , and I didn't want to impose my dog on anyone. But I missed his calming influence as I would stand with my back to a wall, gripping Earl's upper arm to protect my left side from people's touch. If I let go of his arm, he sometimes forgot me and drifted away. I would stay against a wall, seeming to ignore friends across the room. I wanted to greet them, and I felt rude. I couldn't walk over to say hello to them because I was afraid to move. To prepare to leave a crowded room, I stood with my back against Earl's chest, then grasped both of his hands and crossed them in front of me. When I did this, Earl's body became a "cloak" around mine, and we walked in step with one another until we were through the nearest door. He went to several parties alone because I felt safer at home.

I worried about going through with November's tour of Petra and Asia. *It's a few months away,* I told myself. *I'll be well by then. I already paid for it; it's too late for a refund. I'll rise above this illness. Buster just turned eleven; he isn't going to be able to take care of me forever. I have to get over this. I have to be well by November.*

"Get over it?" Dr. Joe questioned. "You need to learn how to manage it. You're not going to just 'get over' it."

I felt so frustrated, I picked up a Kleenex box and threw it at him. Then I plopped down onto the floor. I held Buster, who rolled over and gifted me with the "white alligator." I stroked his beautiful white tummy fur while I thought about responding. My idea of "managing" was to never

leave home, except to ride my horse, get my hair trimmed and see the shrink. We had an exercise therapist who came to the house, I did my shopping on line and Cody came over for dinner once a week. I was blessed with a husband who bought groceries, and he was blessed with a wife who did the accounting. I made sure the bills were paid on time and I was a good partner in our business ventures. I ran two houses. I had enough to manage! Besides, I liked staying home. I had spent too many years working in offices, going to business parties, and traveling. "I've earned the right to stay home and look out at my new pool," I told the doctor. "What the hell's wrong with that?!"

"Not a thing. But you know it isn't healthy."

15

Getting Away

By the end of that August, two years had passed since my accident. Earl and I had realized our dream of having an ocean getaway. It was time to spend a month in Quogue with all three of our dogs, so we left Wrex with the house-sitter, hopped into our SUV and headed east. Gracie, Reggie and Buster slept in the back, then bounded out of the car whenever we stopped to change drivers and buy drinking water. We made each stop at a convenience store next to an open field. The dogs chased one another around the field, we all got our peeing accomplished, then the dogs ran back into the car and went to sleep. At each pet-friendly hotel (pre-booked by our wonderful travel agent), they ran around the grounds, returned to us when we called them, and slept next to our bed through the night. They were easier to travel with than our sons had been.

At a stop to stay with friends, we learned how smart these dogs were. Our friends had built a fortress to contain their two Australian Shepherds. Connected to the fort was a four-foot high, latticed wood fence that enclosed a flight of steps, then surrounded an elevated deck attached to their house.

We parked our car in front of the house, hugged our friends, then ran around in the fort with all five excited dogs. Once our "kids" were playing well together, we adults went inside the house for a drink. While we sat and relaxed, Gracie, Reggie and Buster stood by the patio door, eyes fixed on us through the glass.

When Earl went to the car to get our bags, I walked out to help him. In seconds, all three of our dogs were standing next to the car. *Seconds!* Dumbfounded, our friends said, "How on earth did they get out of there?" We all led our dogs back to the fort locked them in again. Then we asked Earl to go to the car once more. The rest of us stood on the deck and watched to see what our dogs did.

They did geometry! Gracie ran to the bottom of the steps. From a sitting position, she sailed over the four-foot fence. Reggie wriggled his sixty-pound body through a five-inch gap between a fence post and a step. Buster stood at the top of the steps, then made a downward broad jump over the fence. *He may be eleven, but he sure isn't old.*

We realized that they would do anything to be with us, and that each of them could escape a proven fortress. On this trip, they expected to be in the car, or with us, every minute. Those were their rules.

Once we were in Quogue, their favorite outing was a run on the beach. I was pleased to see that Buster had no

trouble keeping pace with his much younger friends. Like them, he was full of energy and craved activity.

Fortunately, some of the neighbors had a job for them. These people had a geese problem. Their house was on a peninsula and they had a lawn the size of two football fields. Gaggles of migratory geese loved to camp on their lawn and make a mess of it. Experts had advised them to keep the geese away in September, if they wanted the migration path to change. Border Collies were the best known repellent. So, three times a day, we took our "Geese Police" over to patrol the property. They raced around the vast lawn, gleefully chasing one another. Then, as though they had been trained to repel invaders, they marked the edges of the property as their territory. The geese went somewhere else, and our neighbors were grateful. Buster had another job to add to his résumé.

I was pleased to think my illness was improving. An off-season month in a small village was a vacation from people in hurried motion. The dogs were content to rest in the house while we went out, and I seldom needed Buster to take care of me. Gatherings of friends were infrequent and very small. The golf courses were almost empty and golf isn't a contact sport. The small village grocery store was seldom busy, and I always shopped there with Earl.

However, the market's screen door was on a tight spring. Each time the door snapped closed, it sounded like a gunshot to me. I jumped each time I heard it. *Bang! Look for lemons. Bang! Remember lettuce. Bang! Pay at the counter. Bang!* I couldn't imagine how the employees tolerated that loud noise hundreds of times each day.

I asked the cashier, "How can you work with that door

constantly making that banging noise?"

"What banging noise?"

I wasn't ready to declare myself "well."

When it was time to leave Quogue, Earl and I were sad, but the dogs were delighted to spend four more days in the car.

After we arrived home, I started to prepare for my international trip. I was rested, organized and ready to go someplace new. But I wasn't sure I could manage it.

Three weeks away, without Buster or Earl? I could stand that, I told myself. I knew I was going to be with people who could help me when I needed it. *If I offend someone, I'll never see that person again, anyway. I'll only be with them for three weeks. I'll get through this. This will help me get well. I have to get out and do things. I have to manage this.* Mind over fright—like getting back on a horse.

On first day of the trip, my outgoing flights were on Halloween, six weeks after 9/11/01. I was grateful the airports weren't crowded; almost nobody was flying that day. I managed my fear of people by getting on each plane early, and getting off last. During the tour, I avoided group meals. Most of our day trips were in small groups of ten, in the countryside, amid ruins. To protect my left shoulder, I kept a huge purse pressed against it. In cities, we were always in comfortable tour buses. I was able to see the world and avoid being bumped into by the people who belong in it.

Between activities, I stayed in my room sleeping, reading, eating protein bars, phoning Earl, and watching American TV news. In hotel lobbies, I kept my back to walls wherever I could find them, and I took only one walk the entire time.

That walk was with someone who uplifted my heart forever. We were in Tibet, on top of the world. It was a warm, sunny day in mid-November—unheard of in the Himalayas. I kept him on my left as we strolled through Lhasa, from the sacred Potala Palace to our hotel. As we walked, we "surfed" each other's minds and souls. After hearing about my accident, he suggested I do some body work because, he noticed, I still moved as if I was hurting. Knowing that Santa Fe is a Mecca for the healing arts, he recommended Rolfing.

"It's soft tissue manipulation," he said. "It realigns your body so it moves in proper harmony again."

Then we chatted about our spiritual histories: devotion to various sects of Buddhism and Christianity, dalliances with astrology, fascination with things weird and not so very. He told me that his childhood in the Texas panhandle had not included much philosophical depth. "If my brothers and I did something terribly naughty, my mother simply said, 'It's all right, God loves you. Now let's have cookies.'"

His words hit me like shower of light. Years of stress and anxiety lifted away. When I returned home, I scheduled an appointment with a Rolfer, and told Dr. Joe about my friend's wonderful remark.

"And?" he said. "Why did that move you so much?"

I was sitting on his couch. Buster sat on the floor, looking up at me. His eyes seemed to ask the same question.

"I don't know. It just woke me up."

"Simple images," Dr. Joe recounted. "A mother says, 'It's all right. God loves you. Now, let's have cookies.' So unlike the mother you had. What do those pictures say to you?"

I glanced at Buster, hoping he could help me with the answer. He looked up at me and smiled, then he wriggled a little and put his paw on my knee.

"It means I'm okay. I'm responsible for my own happiness. I need to mother myself. I need to look to myself to feel nurtured. Nobody else can do that for me."

Buster jumped onto the couch, and started licking my face.

"Good," my doctor said. "It also means, 'Trust the Process."

Then he ducked to avoid another hurled Kleenex box.

16

Embracing Our Obstacles

arl and I spent the holidays with Cody, only. I was tired from my trip, and glad to be home. I welcomed the new year, confident my PTSD was almost over. *I do not have a permanent illness,* I insisted to myself. *I'm going to get through this.*

After the holidays we went to New York City for a small political event in someone's private home. I decided not to take Buster. *How could you?* I was afraid he wouldn't be welcome.

Also, I couldn't stand the thought of leaving Buster alone in a hotel room while we attended the event. *What might he do to try and get out?* And, I wanted to protect *him* from all those big city crowds. Earl could take care of me, I told myself. We were going to be together every second. *I'm getting better. I'm not going to need any help. I can manage.*

I managed to almost draw Earl's blood, as I gripped his upper arm. Walking on the busy New York sidewalks, I tried keeping my body between the buildings and Earl, but I still encountered hundreds of hurrying people. My body felt threatened by each of them. "You grew up in New York," I scolded myself out loud. "You commuted through subway traffic every day at rush hour. You've elbowed through thousands of people at two presidential Inaugurals." We stayed in our hotel room most of the time, where I bristled whenever Earl tried to hug me without warning. We went out, only by taxi, to have a few meals with friends, in restaurants where I was able to sit with my back to a wall. At a Broadway matinee, I edged through the lobby, keeping my back to the walls and taking each step sideways, like a giant crab.

We were the first guests to arrive at the political event, and the last to leave. Fortunately, the gathering was held in a small living room. I could keep my back protected and still have the confidence to be charming.

But I ran out of charm on the flight home. Because of the terrorist attacks that past September, and another plane crash a few months later, New York airports were on extreme alert. After Earl and I made it through the long security line and arrived at our boarding gate, we learned the flight had been delayed. "Please remain in the boarding area and listen for further instructions," the gate agent commanded.

We had left our hotel over an hour before and hadn't had time to stop at a rest room on our way to the gate. I was afraid to find one by myself, and Earl couldn't leave the gate area with me because one of us needed to listen for informa-

tion. Okay, I'm not well enough to travel without Buster, I admitted to my stubborn self. *If he was with me, I could go out into that bustling main aisle and look for a rest room. I miss him desperately.* An hour and a half later, we boarded the plane.

The flight attendants were edgy, which I understood. They had probably lost friends on the planes that crashed, and were still traumatized. However, I was a woman over fifty with an aching bladder just as old. So, I moved toward the rest room when the last few passengers were boarding. A flight attendant shouted, "Return to your seat, Ma'am."

"I really need the restroom," I replied, embarrassed to say that out loud.

"Ma'am. Sit down, and fasten your seat belt. You can get up after we're airborne."

I just kept on walking. "Some day you'll understand," I told her.

I returned to my seat (mission accomplished) well before every passenger's carry-on bag was stowed. The flight attendant smiled at me before she sat down.

In those tense times, she could have had me thrown off the plane for disobeying her order.

"I told you so," Buster seemed to say when we arrived home. When he saw me, he wriggled and whined with excitement. That night, his whine sounded sadder and his need for me to cuddle him seemed stronger. He had missed me, of course, but I'm sure he had worried about me too. When I awoke in the middle of the night, I heard Buster's "Hhuff, hhuff, hhuff," coming from the floor beside me. "Hhuff, hhuff, hhuff," I replied in the dark. "Hhuff, hhuff,

hhuff," he said again. Then we both went back to sleep.

The following week, I needed him to escort me to Los Angeles for two days. I had grown up in New York, Beverly Hills, and Malibu. As part of my determination to return to a normal life, I had planned to visit old friends. Guessing that none of them would welcome Buster as a houseguest, I booked us into a small hotel near the brain-wave therapist.

Before leaving home, I arranged a dinner date with my stepmother, the actress Ann Rutherford. She was a delightful person and I loved seeing her. But I could only meet her on the evening we arrived, the one night I was going to be in Beverly Hills. Knowing Buster would be tired after the plane flight, I planned to let him sleep in the unfamiliar rental car while I was in a restaurant.

"I only eat at La Scala or Trader Vic's," my stepmother said over the phone. In her day, she had starred in countless Andy Hardy movies as Mickey Rooney's perky girlfriend, then she was a tireless wife to my clever father. She had earned her preferences. "But you can't get a reservation at La Scala," she added. "They don't do reservations."

"I'll make a reservation at Trader's," I said.

"We have to be in one of the ship rooms. Your father would only eat in one of those rooms. At one of those tables against the wall."

"Fine with me."

I called her back. "I called Trader's. They're closed that night, and I'm going to be way out in Malibu the next night."

"Then let's go to La Scala. We have to be there by six or we won't get a booth."

"I can't get there by six. My plane lands at five."

"Getting there at six is the only way anyone can get a booth. I don't like the open tables, and I don't want to wait for a booth."

"My plane lands at five. I won't be there by six, but I'll get there as soon as I can."

"Then I'll have to get a friend to come with me. We'll sit in a booth and wait for you."

I wanted to spend the time visiting with my loving stepmother, not getting acquainted with someone new. "I don't want you to go to all that trouble," I told her. "Let me call you back in a few minutes."

I phoned the restaurant. I was learning to function in public and still protect myself. I churned up a mound of courage and said, "I'm calling as a courtesy. I'm planning to dine with you tomorrow night. I have a disability, and I'll be bringing my service dog. I'm letting you know ahead of time, so you can accommodate us both."

"We don't allow dogs."

"My dog is a service dog. I have a disability."

"Sorry. No dogs."

"He's a medical dog. He takes care of me, so I can live a normal life."

"That's our policy, Ma'am. No dogs. Sorry."

I tried not to cry, tried not to give up, and decided to speak up for my needs. "I have a disability. My service dog is allowed in restaurants by federal law."

"Ma'am, you're going to have to call our main office and ask permission."

Now I was irritated. I stayed calm, then said, "It would be best if you call your office and inform them. I'm letting

you know in advance, as a courtesy." I gave him my phone number and said goodbye.

Two minutes later, the phone rang. It was the main office. The woman was extremely polite. She asked me what time I was coming and exactly which booth I wanted. I asked for the large booth in front so Buster would have enough room under the table. They reserved it for me, for seven o'clock, "with pleasure."

"Okay," I said to my stepmother. "We have the large front booth reserved for seven o'clock. Under my name."

"That's impossible. They don't do that."

"They're doing it." I explained about Buster. Until then, she knew nothing about my PTSD, nothing about my need for a service dog. I could tell she still didn't believe me. *Why would she?* I explained again, and assured her we were promised that large booth.

After getting through the flight, claiming my bag, renting the car, and checking into the hotel, Buster and I walked over to La Scala. I was thankful he was next to me because it was after dark and the sidewalks were more crowded than I had expected. I kept his leash short as we entered the restaurant. Two employees noticed Buster's red jacket. They greeted me nicely and pointed to the large booth they had saved for us. As usual, all the other tables and booths were full. I told them I was waiting for my stepmother, Ann Rutherford Dozier. They knew her well.

"She's sitting over there," the maitre d' said. He pointed to a small booth. There my adorable stepmother sat, with a friend.

I led Buster over to their table and said, "They're saving the front booth for us. Let's move over there. Please.

I need to sit there. I went to a lot of trouble."

"Oh, they need that table for large parties," Ann said. "I don't want to be a bother to them. Besides, we're comfortable here. We've been here since six."

"You didn't believe me." *Bless her considerate heart. Of course she didn't.*

"No. They never take reservations."

"But Buster won't fit under this table. We'll kick him all evening. That's why they're holding that large booth for us."

"We won't kick him. We wouldn't do that. Just sit down and have a drink. Enjoy."

Fine. So much for the courage to defend my needs.

Poor Buster was so tired from traveling, he slept through the entire dinner. To avoid being kicked awake by all of us women, he kept the lower half of his body in the restaurant's narrow aisle. With customary style and grace, every waiter stepped over him, no matter how many plates of pasta were balanced on each tray. Several customers stepped over him, too. Even though we were in glitzy Beverly Hills, nobody seemed ruffled by Buster.

After dinner, Buster and I walked back to the hotel, then cuddled together in our little room. The next morning we walked to the therapist's office for my treatments. My brainwaves looked better and my speech had returned to normal.

During the next day and a half we visited my four closest friends, who lived in different parts of the Los Angeles area. We went for a long walk with each of them. I wanted these friends to meet Buster. They have known me most of my life, before I had much self identity, before I found a

career, before I married Earl, before we all grew into semi-retirement. I had told them about my accident, the PTSD, and how much I adore my beautiful dog. But I wanted them to experience him, to see us together, to hear us huff three times to one another, to know how special he is. I wanted them to understand why I love him so much and what an important part of my life he will always be.

They were all charmed by him and amazed by how fit and well behaved he was. Each insisted we *both* stay with them the next time we came to town. They seemed hurt because I had chosen to stay in a hotel.

One friend asked me to leave Buster out by the pool while we went inside to pour something to drink. But Buster jumped through an open kitchen window to be with me. As I looked at the apologetic expression on his adorable face, I said, "Good boy. It's okay."

"Bring him any time," my friend said. "You can both stay here as long as you want. The property is totally fenced in because of our dog. You can leave Buster here when you go out. He'll stay in the back yard." *Sure he will.* I thanked him.

Even in Santa Fe, Buster's zeal to be next to me had become stronger than ever. I wondered if he was taking his job too seriously. Did he sense I was more vulnerable than I thought I was? At the conclusion of a hotel meeting, I walked around the meeting table so I could leave the narrow room. I was unaware that Buster was still on the other side of the table until I saw him jump up onto it. Then he hopped down to the floor without disturbing a single water glass or piece of paper. He wasn't able to go under the table to follow me; the tablecloth had blocked his way.

Our partners laughed, in awe. One of them asked, "How old is that dog?" "Almost twelve," I answered. "Wow! He's going to live forever."

When we were at home, Buster encouraged me to go out. He followed me around the house and motioned toward the outside door whenever we were in the kitchen. When I opened it, he ran to the garage door and stood there waiting for me. When I told him we weren't going anyplace, he lay down with a heaving sigh of disappointment. When I put on shoes of any kind, he danced with excitement and pranced toward the door. He wanted me to get out into the world, too. He wanted me to get well.

"Will you take care of me always," I asked him one day. His bright brown eyes answered, "Yes."

I knelt down, put my hands on either side of his beautiful face and asked, "Will you stay with me until I get well?" He raised his paws up onto my shoulders and hugged me. I knew that was a promise. It almost made me want to stay ill forever.

He accompanied me on my first visit to the Rolfer, who grew to adore him. Each time they greeted one another, Buster turned his hind end toward the therapist and enjoyed a few moments of deep tissue massage. I had recently begun giving him pills for a tiny bit of arthritis, and the Rolfer knew just where to rub.

On our first visit, the Rolfer could tell I had PTSD by the way I carried myself. "I'm a Vietnam vet," he told me. "I've done a lot of work with people with PTSD. The term was invented in Nam, you know. Before then, it was called 'shell shock.'"

I didn't know that.

"I studied with Peter Levine for a while. He wrote a great book about PTSD called *Waking the Tiger*. You ought to read it."

As the Rolfer massaged deep into my flesh twice a week, he helped me understand what I was experiencing. The slightly painful rubbing evoked memories of every physical injury since my toddlerhood. "Rolfing does that," he explained. "It releases the energy trapped in your body's tissues. The energy comes out with the memories." As he worked, I shared each memory with him. In retrospect, most of my tumbles and accidents seemed amusing. During these treatments, the therapist also educated me about my illness.

"PTSD is a physiological condition, it's not psychological. That means, you can tell your mind not to react to something, but your body still will. It's a reflex to perceived danger, like when your hand gets near a flame. In your case, your entire body flinches."

"But I fell off my horse two and a half years ago. When am I going to get over this?"

"It takes time for the symptoms to appear, and time for them to go away. You're right on schedule."

He described my reactions since the "major trauma" as if I had shared them with him.

"First your physical wounds heal," he explained. "Your mind and body focus all your energy on that. Then you keep your emotions bottled up while you get busy staying busy. But your mind keeps reliving the trauma. You're tense; you think you're in control because you're clamping onto your feelings. Your entire personality becomes like a tight fist. Some people never let themselves

get past that stage. They just stay busy and tight."

While the man was kneading my body, Buster lay on the floor. Whenever I winced in pain, he ran over to the therapy table and put his front paws on my body. "It's okay, Buster," the Rolfer said. "I won't hurt her."

"I'm okay, darling," I assured him. "Hhuff, hhuff, hhuff."

He returned to the floor. "Hhuff, hhuff, hhuff."

"That's my good boy."

After a few visits, Buster relaxed through those moments. But he kept his eye on us to be sure I was safe.

The Rolfer continued to educate me. "When people stop forcing themselves to stay busy, they let that guard down, they open that tight fist. The mind may not relive the trauma as often. When that guard starts relaxing, the body starts to let itself react to things in its environment: movements, sounds. When this happens, most people put their guard right back up. They try to convince themselves they're in control. You have the courage not to do that."

"As you allow yourself to let go of the mental part of the trauma, you'll notice your body reacting to things more often. You'll think you're getting worse, not better. Don't let those moments scare you; they're a necessary part of the healing process."

So when I jumped back and screamed after someone rushed behind me to help me blanket my horse, I thanked Scully for standing still and told myself to trust the healing process. When a grocery shopper approached Buster and me in the produce section of a supermarket and asked me what my dog was trained to do, my body froze, my hand squished a tomato, my mouth uttered breathy spasms

"huhgh, huhgh," and my intellect told me it was part of the healing process. For an hour after each of these encounters, adrenaline rushed through my system. It wouldn't subside, no matter how much I wanted it to.

"Trust the Process," Dr. Joe kept telling me. He had learned to keep the Kleenex box out of my reach.

17

Sharing Life's Disappointments

That spring I was no longer pondering divorce. I had helped Scully's trainer open her own dog-friendly stable, Cody had started his own business, the Quogue house had a tenant booked for summer, and I was still afraid to turn my back on people. Buster no longer flew five feet into the air to catch his Frisbee; he caught it as it neared the ground instead. He was still eager to play the game with Earl, but he didn't seem to want to play as long. When he caught the Frisbee and just lay on top of it, Earl knew Buster wanted to go inside. Then Earl turned toward the house, and Buster dashed ahead of him, eager to be next to me.

One early summer evening Earl saw a pet astrology book next to the tabloids in the supermarket. He brought it home as a joke. We knew Gracie and Wrex were born in

July, so we read about Cancer pets. The description fit them very well. Scully was born "some time in early May," and he fit Taurus to the capital T. The profile even mentioned how much he loved being rubbed on the neck. Since we had found Reggie and Buster at the animal shelter, we had to guess their birth signs by reading the descriptions. Reggie's long-legged, happy self matched Sagittarius, and a late November birth fit the approximate age he was given at the shelter. The crowd pleasing, handsome Leo description fit Buster, and an August birth matched what we had been told about his age. So we gave him the same birthday Earl had: August fourteenth.

By Buster's twelfth birthday, the airlines had changed the requirements for service animals due to abuse of the law. Among other abuses, a woman had brought a pig on an airline and said it was her service animal. So any passenger who used a service animal for a disability that wasn't obvious had to carry a recent letter from a doctor who was treating that disability. Any airline employee could ask for the letter, if in doubt about the need for the animal. To protect the traveler's privacy, the letter did not have to name the disability. Dr. Joe was happy to write one for me.

Because of Buster, my disease felt less like a cage. If I was afraid to go somewhere and my husband was busy, I knew I could take my service dog with me. If I panicked when someone approached me, I seldom felt embarrassed. My behavior simply illustrated why I needed my dog. He came with me when I went out to mail packages, to go to a small grocery store, to ride Scully at his new riding stable, to Dr. Joe's, the Rolfer, the chiropractor and the hairdresser. Those were the places I went—that was "getting out." In

public, people seemed neutral toward Buster's presence. But I couldn't miss some comments said loud enough for me to hear them.

"That woman's blind," a mother misinformed her children.

"What the hell's a 'service dog'," one macho beer drinker snickered to another. I kept my mouth shut, but handed him a pamphlet.

"She should get herself an ugly, mean looking dog so people won't try to pet him," scoffed a woman in front of me on an airport jetway. I wanted to snap at her, but I urged Earl to move ahead and walk between us. *The woman wants to see ugly and mean?*

Those comments were unnecessary and meant to be hurtful. We don't remark about wheelchairs, canes or walkers, so there is no need to comment about a service dog. By definition, any disability makes it difficult go out in public. Trying to cope with comments only makes it worse. Vocal criticism is demoralizing, and bullies love to target differences we can't change. But each of us is likely to be afflicted with some sort of disability, if only for a few weeks. A sudden mental disability can be caused by many things, even a death in the family. A sudden physical disability can result from surgery, aging, illness, a stroke or a sudden accident. In seconds, any of us or someone we love might become part of a growing minority, without choice or prior experience. Among other priceless lessons, my disability taught me to have confidence in most people's kindness, and to ignore the criticism of a few.

When we returned to Quogue that September, the owner of the local riding stable let me exercise an old gelding. Buster led our way along a tree-laced, woodland trail. The stable owner was very welcoming to Buster, and I didn't see any reason to tell her he was a service dog. Because the barn was often busy with anxious little children and their adoring parents, Buster's loving presence helped me stay calm. But the barn assistant tried to discourage his visits. "This barn has a cat that attacks dogs," she said.

"I have one of those at home," I replied. "They chase each other all the time."

"But our cat really goes after dogs."

"So does mine. He's used to that."

"I don't want your dog to get hurt."

"Thanks."

Every once in a while, the cat hissed at Buster and stuck his claws out at him. Buster ignored these affronts. The owner and I laughed. The two of them were funny together.

After enjoying our time at the stable, Buster and I usually returned to the house. Because it was our second home, he was comfortable there. I often left him alone to rest while I golfed with Earl. One day we were at our golf club when a dear friend arrived with another man. Since he had been instrumental in our admission to the club, our friend took pride in introducing us to fellow members. When Earl greeted the men, the assistant pro was helping me with my putting grip.

My head was down, my eyes were focused on my putter, when I felt two strong hands suddenly grasp the

back of my neck. A shriek exploded from my mouth as I dashed for the nearest wall.

"Are you all right?" our friend asked. He had been the convivial gripper.

I thrust my hand out toward him in a "stay away" gesture. I was barely able to say, "I need a minute."

"Do you want me to call an ambulance?" the assistant pro shouted.

"I need a minute. No. Thanks. I need a minute."

I was relieved to see Earl comforting our friend, who looked shocked, red-faced, hurt and apologetic. After a few minutes, I had enough control to go to him. Although I had confided my disability to him and his wife (including why and how Buster traveled with me), I knew it was hard for them to believe I had a serious illness. They had only seen me at little dinners or at small cocktail parties, where I always kept my back against a wall, a sofa, or a table.

I hugged our friend and said, "It wasn't you. It's me."

He cautiously returned the hug, trying to touch me as little as possible. "I'm so sorry," he said. "I honestly had no idea."

"I know. It's okay. Now you know." I introduced myself to his companion, then asked them to tee off ahead of us.

My golf skills were hopeless that day. It took two hours to regain my stability. I was depressed to realize there was no "safe" place for me. I was trembling, and adrenaline was surging through my system while Buster was napping in the house.

The house was Buster's vacation home, too. Each

morning, he accompanied Earl on his walk to the village market. On the way, they made a regular stop at a construction business next to the market. The office manager always gave Buster a cookie. He had trained her to greet him at the door when he arrived, and to break the cookie into small pieces for him. "He always takes the cookie from my hand so politely," she told me. "He isn't like the other dogs who come here. He's a gentleman."

Once in a while, we all took a relaxing ride in Earl's boat. Because of Buster's mild arthritis, we boosted him into the boat instead of letting him jump in. I held him close to me as we were rowed across the bay and down the canals. As usual, I loved to feel his body quiver with excitement whenever a bird swam by us. As I watched him thrust his head in the bird's direction, I knew his eyes were locked on it. He adored being on the water and I adored watching him. I wanted him to have as much fun as possible, every minute we had left together. *"…well past fifteen."*

18

Making Memories

To help make Buster's Quogue vacation a little more pleasant, I began to negotiate a truce with that barn cat. Like most male cats, he was very affectionate. He greeted me each time we arrived at the barn. He rubbed against my legs, asking me to pick him up and hold him.

"Be nice to my Buster," I cooed to him. "Please. He takes care of me. He's my best friend, and I love him. So, stop hissing at him. Will you do that for me?" The cat's impish green eyes looked at me with understanding while I rocked him in my arms.

One morning Buster and I were going on a trail ride with other experienced women riders. We saddled some of the stable's horses, mounted, then rode through the parking area toward the shady woodland trail. Suddenly, I heard a loud hiss and saw a ball of fur come flying out from behind

a car. I heard Buster squeal in pain, then watched him run away from the horses. The cat was stuck on his back. After the cat fell off Buster, he chased him.

I kicked the old horse I was riding, and cantered after them. Buster was running away, the much faster cat pursuing him. I positioned my horse between the cat and my dog, moving him from side to side to keep the cat from running forward. Over my shoulder, I saw Buster run into the neighboring woods, east of the stable. I got off the horse and picked up the cat. The little devil was smiling at me and purring. *He's proud of himself!*

My riding partners' horses were a little shaken. I apologized for not warning them I was cantering off, but they knew I was overcome with maternal instinct. I asked them to continue riding without me. They agreed to look for Buster on the trail while I searched on foot.

I was concerned that he was too frightened of the cat to return to the stable. And we were miles from our house. *He might not know how to get back to the house. It isn't his usual home.* I knew I had to find him before he strayed too far.

I ran to some houses near the stable. An elderly man working in his garden had not seen Buster. People walking on that street hadn't either. I phoned Earl and asked him to come and help because one of us needed to be at the stable in case our boy returned.

I got in the car and drove along the surrounding roads as far into the woods as possible. No luck. I described Buster to a man in a pickup truck who said had seen him near a busy road. The road was west of the stable, far from where I had last seen Buster. I hoped he was circling and

not trying to find his way to our house. The man in the truck told me he would keep searching.

I drove back to the barn and saw Earl standing next to our houseguests' car. He was on his cell phone, continuing an important national conference call. He called to me and pointed in the direction I had seen Buster running. The elderly neighbor was walking toward us with my dog, using a thin rope for a leash. Buster was pulling at the rope, trying to run to me.

I rushed to him, fell on my knees and held him. He was whimpering, and I was sobbing. Then I looked at my hands; they were covered with his blood.

I tried to stay calm while I drove to the animal hospital. Buster was in the back seat, lying very still. I hoped his injuries weren't serious. I was ready to nurse him through anything, anything to keep him alive. I was prepared to delay our trip home, whatever was necessary.

Holding Buster while he lay on the vet's examining table, I begged the Universe not to take him from me — not yet. *I love him so much. He's the love of my life! I still need him and he needs me. Please Universe, please.* Buster looked at me with sad eyes while we cleaned his bloody ear. There was a three-inch gash, deep into his flesh.

"You'll have to leave him overnight," the vet said. I looked at Buster's gentle face. I didn't know how to tell him I was leaving him. *Overnight.* He looked at me, then gently placed his paw on my hand. He understood.

"While he's under, I'll clean his teeth," she said. "You can pick him up at noon."

The next day, when I came to get Buster, he was wearing a huge plastic collar. The megaphone look. He had worn

one before, when a benign tumor was removed from behind his elbow. I knew he hated it.

"Does he have to wear this thing?" I asked the vet.

"It will keep him from scratching his ear."

"But, we're flying home tomorrow. It will really get in the way on the plane."

"You don't want the wound opening on the flight."

Ah, yes.

So that I could take the collar off and put it back on during the trip, I brought a little bag to store it in. I removed the collar before we approached the ticket counter.

While I was standing there, Buster sat down. He put his head down, and used one of his back paws to scratch his wounded ear.

I put my hands on either side of his face. "Don't do that, sweetheart," I said to him. "You mustn't scratch your stitches. Your sore has to heal."

He looked at me, as if to say, "Okay. I won't. I forgot."

We kept the collar off during the entire trip. He never scratched the wound.

19

Maturing Together

fter we arrived home, Buster recovered quickly. Our local Santa Fe vet removed his stitches and my service dog returned to duty. As always, he loved doing his job. Every place we went people usually said hello to him first, then acknowledged me. My chiropractor became so fond of him, he started giving spinal adjustments to both of us.

Because our lives had become less hectic, Earl and I wanted more to do as a couple. So we started riding together. Saturday or Sunday rides on the trail became a family activity—all three dogs ran with us. Buster stayed close to Scully and to Earl's borrowed horse while Gracie and Reggie patrolled our perimeter. I felt almost no fear, even while cantering on a trail. But I still relived the accident each time I drove to the stable.

I was willing to try anything to get well. After I finished my series of Rolfing treatments, I made an appointment to start another form of short-term therapy: Eye Movement Desensitization and Reprocessing (EMDR). I had been told it was the most effective treatment for PTSD. *Until I'm well, I'll get all the therapy I can.*

I wanted to be free of my disease, every bit of it. I wanted to rip my cage apart and throw it away. It was the fall of an election year, and two good friends of ours were running for governor and lieutenant governor. I hated not being able to participate in their campaigns; they had always been there for Earl and me. For over a year, their fund raising teams had asked me to assume the major role I had in past elections, but I was afraid to be in a crowded meeting or in a receiving line at a banquet. Earl didn't belong at my meetings, Buster couldn't protect me from every unexpected friendly touch, and I couldn't control my protective reflexes. So I raised more money than I ever had, by asking a few people to donate a lot. I still had wisdom, but I didn't feel free.

Buster's freedom was restricted too. His arthritis began to slow his pace. He needed pain pills and supplements twice a day. Unless I rolled them into a ball of ground meat, he refused to take them. He turned his nose away and looked insulted. At the vet's suggestion, I started to squirt canned cheese on the pills. He loved it. Soon, he started to con me into giving him extra cheese by licking it off the capsules. *That rascal.*

The new recipe helped both of us because it started an important ritual. Every morning and late evening, Buster began to interrupt whatever I was doing. To get my atten-

tion, he batted my hand with his nose. Then he looked up at me, pricked his ears, let one ear droop slightly and licked his chops. It took me a few weeks to realize what he was telling me: "It's time for my arthritis pills and for your hormone replacement pills." We were maturing together.

As the election neared, I felt eager to have more activity. My energy was returning and I wanted to do something that could make a lasting difference. My ability to function in groups was limited, but I had a lot of time. So I decided to put an end to a public eyesore.

Santa Fe's central square, its Plaza, has been a gathering place for centuries. It is on the National Register of Historic Places. But for almost twenty years the city allowed an ugly plastic and stainless steel performing stage to dominate it. On summer and early fall weekends the stage was used for civic or political rallies, band concerts and dance recitals. The rest of the year it was a useless hulk. To avoid state and local building restrictions, plus the ADA requirements, the city called their stage a "temporary" structure. I was one of many Santa Feans who were disgusted by it. So I gathered a group of wise friends to create something worthy of our historic and beloved Plaza.

Over the next few months, we met in small rooms (my choice) and developed a new stage. For the first time in anyone's living memory, we were proposing a permanent structure for the Plaza. We hired the state's leading history-sensitive architect to draw a plan. To protect her design, we decided not to ask for public funding. I often repeated my favorite description of a camel: a horse designed by a civic committee. Our Plaza is nostalgically sacred and we knew the stage was going to take years to complete. We

had to navigate through layers of bureaucracy, raise a lot of money, and be a glacier of persistence.

Some members of my team were skeptical, but I wasn't daunted. A few of us were veteran fundraisers, and I had experience with persistence. I was ready to be the "sheepdog" for the project. It was my job to keep everyone united and moving forward. I thought about the obstacles I had overcome since my accident, and knew I wouldn't give up. Having a disability had made me a wiser and more patient person, and was going to teach me more.

After he turned thirteen, Buster's hind legs could no longer let him stand up to hug me. So I started kneeling down to hold him. When he lay down on the floor, I often curled up next to him so we could hug one another.

When he first needed my help getting up onto the bed, I wanted to cry. I lay on top of the covers with him and said, "Please stay with me. I love you so much. Please stay with me until I'm well." I began to turn to the Universe daily. I asked it to keep us healthy and thanked it for letting Buster stay with me so long. *I can't imagine going through life without him.*

"He has also kept you in your marriage," Dr. Joe said. "He's provided you with affection and companionship. Without Buster, you might have looked for it someplace else. In another relationship, maybe."

"EMDR really isn't about the movement of the eyes,"

the social worker explained. "It helps our mind re-process past experiences."

As I scanned the eclectic assortment of wall decorations in her office, she continued to explain the process.

"Some researchers say PTSD can build over time. We all have traumas throughout life. Some people are more emotionally sensitive than others. Or, one episode can unleash the stress someone's been holding in from other traumas for years."

When we were ready to begin the treatment, she reached for a small drum and asked me to talk about an accident. "Not your horse accident. Something earlier. Go back as early as you can remember."

I took a deep breath, and thought for a minute. Then I said, "I was six. I was watching my mother cook dessert."

Drum. Drum. Drum. When she started beating that drum, Buster gave me a startled look. He opened his mouth, and seemed to be laughing. I was trying not to.

"I looked into the chafing dish, and watched my mother pour kerosene on the flame."

Drum. Drum. Drum.

"All of a sudden, I saw my stepfather lunging toward me. His eyes were wide and he looked crazy."

Drum. Drum. Drum.

"He threw me down onto the floor, and rolled on top of me."

Drum. Drum. Drum.

"I was terrified. I couldn't breathe."

Drum. Drum. Drum.

"My hair had caught on fire. He put the fire out."

Drum. Drum. Drum.

"My face was burned. We rushed to the hospital."

"Good," she said. "Now, live that experience again. This time let the fire flare up slightly, not enough to burn you. Let's see what happens."

I relived the experience again, and again. Each time, she asked me to modify the memory. Drum. Drum. Drum. Soon, the experience became a very pleasant evening: a happy family making peach flambé.

During each session we worked through another memory, another childhood injury. *Traumas*. We were saving the fall from Scully for last.

My Elder Statesman

As we were leaving to go riding one Sunday, Gracie and Reggie were leaping with excitement. Earl was wearing his riding boots, and we were walking toward the SUV. They could tell they were going riding with us. We could almost hear them saying, "Yes, yes, yes! We get to go, we get to go!" Buster was not thrilled. He lay on the front patio, sunning himself. He looked at me as if to say, "I'm getting too old for this trail riding stuff. Take them."

"Are you sure you want to stay home, my smoochie poochie?" I asked him. "All by yourself?"

He rolled over and presented me with the "white alligator." I rubbed his tummy.

"We're home now, not in Quogue. There's no attack cat at this barn."

Buster returned to his former relaxed position and looked at me. "I'll be fine," his eyes seemed to say. "I know you'll be back." He put his head down and rested.

Starting that day, Buster stayed home while Gracie and Reggie came on Sunday rides with us. They rocketed along miles of trails while I rode Scully, and Earl rode an old horse we borrowed for him. I no longer feared cantering and galloping; I thrived on it. The thrill of speed was a good emotional release for me.

But late one dark afternoon, Scully shied while we were galloping. I lost my balance for a second, and my right foot slipped out of its stirrup. As I wriggled my foot to recover the stirrup, I was afraid I was going to fall. By the time I had slowed Scully to a trot, I decided that a little bit of fear was healthy protection. *No more galloping; he can gallop in his corral without me.*

But a little cantering on the open trails with Earl was fun. Gracie and Reggie were good protection, and they loved their long runs with us. Buster remained content to stay home; he had become an elderly statesman.

Other statesmen were doing well also. Our friends were elected Governor and Lieutenant Governor by an impressive margin. The inaugural ceremonies were six weeks after the election and I was asked to "chair something." I felt eager to help, but I was still afraid. I hadn't screamed in public in several months, but I dreaded that I might. *Crowded meetings, balls, ceremonies — Drum. Drum. Drum.*

So I chose to be in charge of the written program. I had done the same job for a previous governor and knew how much stress was involved. The task involved a few small meetings, no large groups, and it would "wrap" before

Christmas. The progress on the Plaza stage was slow, so I had time for another project. I also had the stamina. *I can do hard work. I have energy now!*

I worked under tremendous time pressure every day and night for over a month. Gathering and editing lists and schedules for a program required constant herding by phone, fax and e-mail. Buster helped me get through the stress. As always, he lay by my side while I worked at my desk. He also came to every meeting and stayed behind my chair. I was no longer concerned that a uniformed service dog made me look "weird." People were either my friends, or they weren't.

After one meeting, while Buster was leading me through a door, a fellow volunteer grabbed me from behind to tell me something. I let out a short squeal, not a terrifying shriek. But I recovered quickly. *Drum. Drum. Drum.*

"Sorry about that," I said to her. "I'm still getting well. This is why I need my dog."

She understood.

The printed program was lovely, but I stayed home during the Inaugural ceremonies. Earl and I went to one ball, for less than an hour. Again, I "cloaked" his body around mine the entire time.

When I felt the stress of my projects, I tried to stay calm. To escape the pressure some days, I cantered Scully on a short trail that was visible from the stable. Because people could see me if I fell, the trail was safe for riding alone. When I went to the stable by myself, Buster came with me. But I didn't expect him to run on the trail. I asked him to wait in the car while I rode my horse. He seemed content to have the rest, and getting him into the car was

a ritual he and Scully loved. I mounted Scully, moved him next to the car, then reached down and opened the door. After Buster hopped inside, I pushed the door closed and pressed the lock button on my key. When I returned from my ride we repeated the process and Buster hopped out. Then, with a big smile and his tail in the air, he led Scully and me back to the barn.

When I was grooming my horse, Buster enjoyed protecting me in the barn. He never frightened a stable worker; he just made it clear he was there for me. When I schooled Scully in the outdoor arena, Buster lay near the perimeter and watched us. When I dismounted in the middle of the arena, he left his resting spot and pranced over to us. His body twisted with joy, and his smile told me he was glad I was safe. He was ready for my attention again.

"Good boy," I said to him. "Show me the way." He knew those words meant he should walk in front of me, not next to me. He trotted forward, giving little looks back to make sure I was following him to the barn.

At home, Buster was having more trouble getting onto the bed. He made a running leap, got his body up, but his lower legs didn't spring him high enough. He would slide to the floor, land with a thud, and heave a disappointed sigh. Then he would look up at me, mortified. He didn't seem to like being boosted either. Maybe it hurt him, maybe he felt undignified. So I sent away for a set of steps, and kept them at the foot of the bed.

But Gracie had become the queen of the lower half of our mattress. Whenever Buster would start to approach "her half" of the bed, she would growl at him. So I sat next to the steps to be sure he could climb them with dignity. *Protection works both ways.*

However, I had to function without his protection during an important event. In January we presented our stage plan to Santa Fe's Historic Design Review Board, then showed it to the City Council. The review board voted to approve it and the council applauded it. Our group of founders was celebrating, but a long battle had begun.

I decided not to take Buster to those public hearings. I didn't want to call attention to myself. Since Earl was a successful real estate lawyer, approvals had once been his forté. Half a decade had passed since I had sat with him at civic meetings, and the councilors up on the podium didn't know I was recovering from an injury. *They're going to wonder why I have the audacity to bring my dog to their meeting.* I needed my husband there as an advisor, but success like his is sometimes resented. I wanted us to seem invisible. Our project was to be a gift to community, not another win for Earl.

We also needed Earl to "work" the participants and the spectators. I didn't want him to focus on me. So, I asked Cody to be my "service person." He let me hold his arm, seemed to know better than I did which doors were safest for me to pass through, and was my loving protector. I was very proud of my thoughtful son.

Buster did come with me on most of my visits to raise funds. Even though I'm good at asking people for big donations, I was afraid to walk from my car to their offices. Since Buster's favorite thing in life is parading in public (one of his Leo traits), he was delighted to prance by my side.

I was also afraid to go to the Academy Awards ceremony. That year my beloved aunt, Olivia de Havilland, two-time Oscar winner "Melanie" in *Gone With the Wind*, was making an appearance. She wanted me to be in the audience. But I knew the crowds would make me feel apprehensive and agitated. *You have to be there for her. She's eighty-five years old. This could be her last Oscar show.*

My aunt was flying all the way from her home in Paris, and she deserved what she wanted: her daughter, her agent, a close family friend, my husband and me enjoying the evening with her. But I was planning to fly to Los Angeles all the way from Long Island, and I didn't want to have a miserable time. I told her I loved her, but I just didn't want to suffer those jostling crowds. Very understanding, she arranged for us all to have brunch in her hotel suite the morning after the show. We also attended a small dinner in her honor at a private home. I survived my travel anxiety by keeping my back to walls and clinging to Earl in hotel lobbies and airports. Those meals with my aunt and my dear cousin will always be treasured memories. I know I'll forget the anxiety, some day.

After we returned from Los Angeles, Earl and I went to Target to have some photos from the trip enlarged. While we were leaning over the self-serve photo machine, someone grabbed my left shoulder. I heard her voice say, "And what are *you* doing here?"

I screamed, several times, then saw the startled face of a sweet friend from old political campaigns. She was agog. Beyond her, dozens of Target shoppers and associates stood staring at me. Two seconds of silence. They went right back

to what they were doing, but my friend was obsequiously apologetic. Adrenaline rushing, throat tight, limbs weak, I buried myself in Earl's arms. All I could say to her was, "Please go. Please go." I phoned her the next day and explained my behavior. Clearly, Buster's job wasn't over. I still had a lot of healing to do.

"What is it about focus?" Dr. Joe asked me. "You were focused on something. She interrupted you. Is focus about control?"

"Probably."

"And what happens when you're afraid of losing control?"

Drum. Drum. Drum. The EMDR therapist took me back through the memory. "Let's do it again. This time, imagine her coming over to you and her touch means friendship."

"It did! It did mean friendship. That's why I feel so awful. I don't want to scream at another friend again."

"So. Are you afraid of the fear?"

I held Buster close to me, then answered her.

"Right. I am. I'm terrified of being frightened."

"Okay. Let's begin the exercise. Let go of Buster, for now."

Drum. Drum. Drum.

Soon, I was gaining more confidence in public. When we went to small parties, I no longer had to keep my back against heavy furniture. I could go to mini grocery stores without much anxiety. When doing quick errands I often left Buster in the car, knowing I could get him if I was afraid.

But trying to function without him was a sad experi-

ment. I was testing my new confidence by leaving my adorable friend behind. He lived for his job; he thrived on taking care of me. I couldn't take his job away from him. I wanted him beside me, but knew I had to prepare for a future without him. *...well past fifteen.* He was in perfect health—just a little arthritis. *Oh, please, Universe, please keep him with me.*

I continued to kneel down and ask Buster, "Please stay alive until I get well." He would look at me with those gentle brown eyes. Then he would put his paw on my shoulder, to assure me. His job was giving us both a life.

I felt guilty when I agreed to another Asian trip. Earl and I planned to be gone for most of November. *I can't leave Buster for three weeks.* The trip was to be in honor of Earl's sixtieth birthday. *Maybe I'll be well. It's nine months away.* Our marriage had survived tremendous strain. My husband had coped with my suffering, and he deserved a lot of attention. We needed a romantic adventure together. *What will my darling Buster do without me? His heart could break while I'm gone.* My conscience told me I had to put my marriage first. But, without Buster with me, I had trouble surviving even one spring day in Texas.

Our retail business was leasing a store on San Antonio's River Walk. Our managing partner deserves our opinions and support, no matter what. So we had to go there and look at the space with him. It was an overnight trip and I decided to try traveling without Buster.

After mid-morning, the River Walk is teeming with thousands of strolling tourists. Feeling anxious the entire time, I clutched Earl's arm when we walked to and from the

site. I kept him on the left side of my body, the edge of the river on the right. I looked down at the murky water and imagined myself stumbling into it. I couldn't get home to my precious puppy soon enough.

We took Buster to Quogue that June. Earl and I needed to get the house ready for that summer's tenants. I had several errands to do, so there was plenty of work for all three of us. Buster no longer ran ahead of Earl on their morning walks to the village. He now walked by his side. As always, the "cookie lady" was delighted to see him. He no longer ran after birds on the beach, but he still trotted ahead of us and pranced in the water. I stopped taking him to the horse barn; it belonged to that fiendish cat. He took more naps than ever before, but when he was awake he followed me up and down the stairs and from room to room, never letting me out of his sight. When I lay on the upstairs balcony's double chaise, he lay next to me.

One day as Buster and I lay on that chaise together, I thought about how much I loved feeling his body next to mine. Almost four years had passed since my accident. I still wasn't comfortable when Earl touched me, and I felt anxious about being touched by other people. But I craved the tender, sensitive touch of my animals. Hugging my horse, my dogs or my cat made me feel cherished and nurtured. Between us there was a radiant warmth that flowed through our point of connection. Tension left my body and life seemed simple and safe. Holding them calmed me more than a sip of a strong drink did, or melodies of smooth music, or the sound of the ocean. Was this because Scully and my pets seemed to "ask" before touching me; because they didn't expect anything in return; because their touch

was never threatening or controlling? I wasn't an expert about anything. But I knew I felt loved and complete while cuddling with my darling Buster.

I gazed out over the grassy green wetlands, toward the brilliant blue bay. I thanked the Universe for our breathtaking environment, and for allowing my beautiful Buster to share it with me. He put his head on my chest, then snuggled closer to me. We huffed three times and nuzzled one another. Together, we were in heaven.

On another mild and sunny weekday, Earl and I drove to Sagamore Hill, Theodore Roosevelt's Long Island museum and former residence. Expecting it to be crowded, we brought Buster with us. Luckily, only a few other visitors were there that day. Buster scampered through the apple orchard, was welcome in the air-conditioned museum, and was part of our small group tour through the residence.

The other members of the group were very polite to us. Having a dog in the historic house made it seem more like a home. As always, Buster received many compliments for being so well behaved and good looking. When we went upstairs, each bedroom was roped at its entrance so we could see inside without touching anything. When we came to the bedroom that had once belonged to the late president's daughter, Alice Roosevelt Longworth, I noticed a tiger rug on its floor. A Bengal tiger, with a mouthful of huge teeth. Buster walked to the edge of the rope barrier with me and gazed into the room. Then he thrust his head forward toward the tiger rug and fixed on it. He crouched down and uttered a long, low growl. "He's protecting us from that tiger," I explained to everyone.

Some relaxation and a little presidential culture was good for our small family, because I had a big project waiting in Santa Fe. Our governor had asked me to organize a dinner for the former president, at our home. The governor had promised to raise money for the president's library and knew he could count on me to help him raise it. To meet his monetary goal and make the dinner price affordable, I realized I needed to seat a hundred and thirty guests. *A lot of people in motion!*

Raising the money didn't dissuade me, nor did arranging for the tables, the outdoor tent, or the catering. Typing long lists was a pain, but part of the process. *Trust the Process.* I had dealt with the Secret Service and political advance people before; I was prepared to absorb the stress they imposed. Only two things daunted me: I didn't want publicity, because I didn't want some wacko poisoning my dogs. And I didn't want to be elbowed by all those people. Not in my own back yard.

On the evening of the party I spent the start of the cocktail hour visiting with close friends. It was a joy to see each person again. I had been away from them for years, and I felt happy to be entertaining them. When the area began to feel crowded, Buster and I walked to the front of the house and stood behind the reception table. (At the caterers' request, Reggie, Gracie and Wrex were encamped in the study, to keep them away from the food.) When the president arrived he greeted our family, then he went into the house for a short break.

I went back out to the party to help herd the guests

to their seats. Standing at my assigned table, I turned to watch the guest of honor enter our garden. I watched my husband walk across the lawn with the former President of the United States. While they were chatting, they didn't notice Buster leading them toward me, showing them the way.

As hostess, it was proper for me to sit next to the president. The tables were round and I didn't want my back to anyone. When planning the seating, this had been a big worry for me. I knew I would be nervous just trying not to sound stupid while talking with this very intelligent president. *But how am I going to protect my back from people who want to come to our table and chat with him?* I found a solution the Secret Service loved: I put the president's table in a corner, his seat and mine in front of a fat, prickly pine tree. As a result, the people at our table had an uninterrupted conversation with the president. When it was time for him to make his speech, he took the cordless microphone to the middle of the space and was brilliant for over an hour. When the president thanked me for organizing the event, he told me the dinner had been a lot of fun for him.

The next morning I looked back on our party's successes. The weather was perfect, we raised more money than expected, everyone had a great time, our hotel did a perfect job of catering, and I made sure the valet parking kids had a group photo taken with the president. Best of all, I had a good time! *Trust the Process.* I was in top form, my old self—a capable and gracious person. I even enjoyed hugging people. I felt proud. I knew my father would have been proud of me. But I hadn't paid any attention to Buster. After watching him lead the president into the garden, I

don't know where he went. He didn't enter my mind. I was sad to realize I had forgotten all about my closest friend. *How could you?*

When we took Buster to Quogue that September, he had become even slower. He wasn't jaunty on the walks to the village, but his pace quickened in cool weather. When I went jogging, he stayed next to me, but twenty minutes of running exhausted him. A long leap didn't get his hind legs onto our bed there either, so I bought him another set of steps.

But I wasn't sleeping well. One of our Santa Fe city councilors was determined to kill the Plaza stage project. I felt so depressed, I wanted to give up. *But we've already raised most of the money!*

When the architect phoned me to describe each arrow the councilor was shooting, Earl and I made phone calls to other officials to try and stop the bleeding. Each day there was another wound. The councilor's maneuvers required the project to be argued at a public hearing, and he was gathering troops to battle against it. Earl and I had to organize a planning meeting, recruit troops for our side, and fly home to keep the project alive.

The hearing was intense. Our lovely "gift horse" was put through root canal surgery. But our troops prevailed and the council didn't reject the project. Instead, they approved a motion to let their staff tinker with its design for a month. A slow death was almost inevitable. I was exhausted when we left the crowded meeting. To protect my body from all those people in motion, I sandwiched myself between

Earl and Cody. When I got inside our car I knew there was nothing I could do. Without a vote for approval, more fund raising was futile. I felt depressed, deflated and useless. So I went home and cuddled with Buster.

A week later, Earl and I left on our long-scheduled Asian trip. We were due back in Santa Fe before the next city council meeting, and all I could do about the Plaza stage was wait. While in Cambodia and Katmandu, I answered the architect's desperate phone messages and reminded her that waiting was our only option. I was grateful to be out of the country. The distance kept my mind off the project.

I managed my disorder on the trip. My back-to-any-thing-at-all habits had become natural, and Earl enjoyed cloaking me with his body in crowds. I snarled at a government official in Beijing when she grabbed me to slow my pace through a metal detector. But she didn't arrest me, and I didn't scream.

When we came home, our house-sitter told me that Buster had not done well at all. Two weeks after we left, she found him lying in the garden, unwilling to move. She couldn't lift him. When she called the veterinary clinic, they sent two assistants and a stretcher. He had a high fever, but they could not find the cause.

"He missed you," Dr. Joe said. "He couldn't do his job."

"He thought I had abandoned him. He was heartbroken."

"Those are your issues from childhood. But, yes, he could well have felt those things."

I knew Buster couldn't go everywhere with me. But I was afraid he might give up on life if I left him for that long again.

I sat on the floor of the Dr. Joe's office and looked at Buster's adorable black and white face. He sat up when I spoke to him. "I promise you, Bussie. I won't do that to you ever again. I love you. Unless you come with me, I'll never go away for more than a week. I'll never abandon you. I don't ever want you to leave me. Not ever. So, please, promise you'll stay here with me." He put his paws around my neck, and hugged me.

21

Cancer in the Family

*E*arlier that year, Cody's girlfriend had been diagnosed with breast cancer. She was determined to remain positive. By the time we returned from our Eurasian trip, she was undergoing chemotherapy and wearing an attractive blonde wig. Despite her uncertain prognosis, she kept working at her two jobs, and remained focused on all the goodness in life. In constant pain, she continued to be very loving toward everyone. I admired her tremendous courage.

Cody was fighting to stay positive, also. His girlfriend's two children are a decade younger than he is. As a family, they seemed to believe that a positive attitude would heal the disease. Several of my friends have overcome cancer, but I haven't had my turn. So I could only try to empathize with her and be sensitive to their suffering.

More than anything, I wanted to comfort Cody. Clearly, he was masking deep fear and sorrow. During our weekly home dinners with him, Earl and I talked about the cancer only when he mentioned it. We assured him we were there for his emotional support and whatever help he needed. When he let a few tears escape his brave mask, I held his hand until he let it go. The adorable, tow headed child who had once cried in my arms had become a thirty-two year old man with a receding hairline and a ponytail. I wanted to hold him and cry with him, but he was no longer asking me for that much mothering. Our sons are men now and we try not to impose our parental feelings on them. When we're asked, we express them without hesitation. Our most important job in life is to be their wise parents and good friends. We wish we could protect them from suffering, but we can't.

Not wanting to spend Thanksgiving Day away from his girlfriend, Cody brought her to our house for dinner. As the four of us ate turkey and stuffing, she was cheerful, fun, and optimistic about her future. She loved being with Wrex and our dogs, and had always been especially fond of Buster.

Compared to hers, my illness was nothing. I still needed to manage it, but I was doing well. When we went to a holiday party at the governor's residence, I was able to visit with people instead of standing in the usual corner with my back against a potted palm. To feel safe, I still had to cling to Earl's arm or keep his body wrapped behind mine. This had become a habit. He had finally learned not to drift away from me and he responded to my gentle directive touches with little hesitation. He and Buster were my

protection team. One took care of me at social events; the other took care of me when I went out alone.

Since Buster could no longer jump into the SUV, I bought a folding ramp for him. But I could tell he didn't like it; it was embarrassing. Whenever we lifted open the rear door, Gracie and Reggie would squeal with excitement, fly through the opening and land in vehicle's back cabin. But Buster would trot toward the car, put his front paws up on the bottom of the rear opening, and give up. He would stand there looking up at us, his eyes filled with disappointment. Always a guardian of his pride, he kept his chin high.

We knew that lifting him was an affront to his dignity, because Gracie would give him a territorial snarl when he entered the space with our help. But when we first unfolded the ramp and secured it in place, Buster tried to jump onto the middle of it. That didn't work either; he fell to the ground. So I held his shoulders and guided him toward the ramp's starting point.

"Here, darling. Walk up the ramp from here. Good boy."

He snorted at me and tried to jump into the car again. Guiding his shoulders once more, I said. "This way. This ramp is just for you. *They* don't get to use it. It's only for you." He walked up the ramp.

After we repeated this coaxing process during two outings, he got it. From then on, he walked up his ramp with regal poise. When we arrived at our destination, Reggie and Gracie would bound out of the car at the first hint of an okay. Buster jumped out too; flying downward was easy for him. "See? I'm not old," he seemed to say. I agreed with him.

The Plaza stage was approved in early December, with no design changes. Our state's first lady, the governor's wife, spoke at the crucial city council meeting. She came there by choice; I hadn't thought to invite her to a city event. And she was stunning. She gave a short, direct speech urging the council to accept "this once-in-a-lifetime" privately funded "jewel" for the historic center of our state's capital city. Her words were just what the councilors needed to hear. Almost all of them voted yes. *Yes!*

The next morning, the city staff advertised a request for construction bids. There was still time to get a contract approved and start building before spring. I was praying for a price we could afford. We had to raise the rest of the money.

I resumed my fundraising visits. Whenever I went to a private home, or to an office with its own parking lot, I asked Buster to rest in the car. I was able to walk through uncrowded places without him, but I wanted him to spend his days with me. I couldn't leave him at home, feeling useless. He needed to work.

Having a job was keeping him alive, I reminded myself. *He promised to take care of me until I'm well. He promised. I promised to take care of him until...forever.*

On the afternoon the construction bids were allowed to be unsealed, Buster came to the meeting with me. He had been by my side at almost every stage meeting, but I particularly wanted him at this one. I needed his calming closeness, because I knew I would be tense. The results of the bids were vital: if we didn't have a builder we could

afford, the project would be delayed at least a year. *Or be killed.*

Seconds before the deadline, I squeezed the architect's fingers and wrapped my arm around Buster. We watched a grim-faced city official enter the room. I held my breath while he read the results: there was only one bid. Having just submitted his bid, that builder was still in the room. He is a great contractor, someone we all know well, and we could afford his price. We could open by the Fourth of July! The architect cried, the city's project manager and I jumped and whooped, Buster barked and wagged his tail, the builder and the fund manager hugged one another. After two and a half years of struggle, we were about to build a little piece of history. One that was accessible to everyone.

Two weeks later, Buster was having trouble getting out of the SUV. When I parked in front of Dr. Joe's office, I had to lift Buster's torso to help him get down his ramp. I called the veterinary clinic, and they found time to see us it at the end of the day. During my therapy session, Buster seemed sad and listless. He refused to drink water. Dr. Joe helped me lift him into the SUV and I let him rest there while I chaired a short meeting for the Plaza stage.

Buster's condition concerned me more than the meeting did. I knew we would get the stage built on time. I had faith in myself, the merits of the project, and the good will of everyone involved. I also had faith in the Universe — I was no longer a crabby pessimist. I ended the meeting as soon as possible, so I could get my best friend to the vet.

When we arrived at the clinic, Buster seemed grate-

ful to be there. He lay very still and looked up at me with thanks. The doctor discovered a high fever and a very sore hind leg. Then he looked for a bite on that thigh and found one. "Probably from another dog," he said.

An X-ray showed that a large abscess had formed under his skin. They needed to operate immediately.

I said good-bye to him, "It's okay, darling. Go with your doctor; he's your friend. Good boy. You're going to be all right. I love you. You're my good boy. Everything's going to be fine." Then I watched the doctor carry him away.

I hated leaving him; I hated not being able to tell him why I was going. I cried while I drove to the pharmacy to fill his pain pill prescription. When I returned to the clinic, I was allowed to go into the back room. Buster was lying on the floor.

"He'll come out of the anesthesia soon," the doctor said. "He's going to be groggy for a while."

I sat on the cold linoleum and petted him, quietly saying, "How's my boy? My beautiful boy. My beautiful Bussie. My good boy."

When his eyes opened, he looked at me and made a squealing yawn. Then he tried to move his legs and couldn't.

"Hhuff, hhuff, hhuff," I said to him.

He huffed twice, then coughed once, almost choking.

"It should take him about half an hour," the doctor said. "Then he'll be able to move normally." He didn't ask if I preferred to sit in a chair. He had known us for more than a decade.

I knelt beside my big groggy puppy and stroked the top of his smooth, black head. "It's okay. We'll be home soon."

Buster looked at me and sighed. His soft eyes were an old man's eyes, his sigh was an old man's sigh. He seemed resigned to being unable to move. He seemed to understand he was getting old.

Because the clinic was closing for the day, I asked the doctor and one of his assistants to put Buster on a stretcher and help him into my SUV. I could tell they wanted to go home. When I brought our old boy home, Earl helped me lift him out of the car and he was able to walk into the house. As to the cause of the infected bite, either Gracie or Reggie had some explaining to do, but that would come later.

Within a week, Buster recovered.

Sadly, Cody's girlfriend did not. Her prognosis was grim, but she continued to stay brave. Dependent on bottled oxygen to breathe, she no longer had enough energy to work. Cody stayed by her side when he wasn't working. They were determined to keep their lives as normal as possible.

Soon the cancer spread to her lungs, forcing her to be moved to the hospital. Cody and her loving family were with her when the disease stole her last breath. After the memorial service was behind him and all the plans for packing her things were made, we asked Cody if we could plan a trip with him. I remembered feeling dangerously despondent after my father died, and I wanted my son to have something to look forward to.

Having fun again seemed unimaginable to him, but he knew he was going to need a rest. So he agreed to let us take him to Costa Rica, for just a week, the only time he expected his business to be slow: early December. We had all year to plan, all year to think about being a family again.

22

Taking Time to Travel

T his isn't fun," my closest friend from childhood said. She and her husband had sold their house in Malibu, and she was packing its contents all by herself (her husband was a procrastinator). She had leased a horse ranch five hours out of the city so she could live out a persistent dream. For thirty years she had been in the Los Angeles area, and a short plane trip had always brought us together. But with their move, traveling to see one another was about to become an ordeal. I wanted to be with her during her last days in the area we had known growing up together. I also wanted to help her with some of that packing.

Buster and I flew to Burbank, landing late at night. We drove to Malibu in a rented Ford, and four dogs bounded out of my friend's house when we arrived. They growled at Buster, who did not growl back. A round of intense sniffing

followed. Then came spurts of cautious tail wagging and lots of ceremonial leg lifting. Soon the dogs allowed Buster into their masters' house, where no other visiting dog had gone before. They each wanted to be his new friend. But when they wanted him to run and play with them, he was too tired from the trip. So tired, he cuddled with me in bed all night and never stirred.

The next day he focused on us women at work, and was tolerant of the other dogs' playfulness.

"Hey, guys," he seemed to say to them. "Don't bug me. I need to stay near my mom."

"Okay," they seemed to reply. "Are you sure? We're really fun. Let's go out and run around and around in the yard. Let's go!"

"Give me a break. I have a job to do. I want to stay here."

"Gee. You're no fun."

"Too bad, kids."

After another night of cuddling, we said good-bye to our friends. Lots of hugs, tail wagging and pitiful faces. While driving over the green Pacific coast mountains toward the Burbank airport, I thought about decades of visits with my friend. *I'm sorry those visits were so short, I wish I had spent more time with her.* Another phase of our lives had passed, and a new one was about to begin. *Our friendship will last forever.* Boarding the plane with Buster, I wondered how much time I still had with him. *Is this our last trip together? Will we have enough time to do this again?* "...well past fifteen."

When we returned home, construction on the Plaza stage had finally begun. I took Buster with me to recruit the last few donors, then started designing the bronze plaque. *In*

fifty years, we'll all be gone, but our names will be on this plaque.
Each donor's name had to be spelled correctly. Some more
modern married couples preferred to use the wife's maiden
name as well as the husband's name, and I listed their names
exactly the way they wanted them. These people had better
stay married, I said to myself. *Will we?*

Again, I felt doubtful about staying in our marriage.
I couldn't understand why I felt that way. I loved and ad-
mired Earl. He had been extremely patient with me, a saint.
We weren't arguing much, he was trying hard to improve
his absent-mindedness, and I had become less jumpy when
he touched me. But when he went to Denver to play golf
with a friend, I was delighted he was gone. Feeling sad and
puzzled, I went to a psychic reader for clues.

She looked at our astrological charts, then dealt some
Tarot cards. "All of you Scorpio women have been in a major
flux for a year and a half," she said. "You're re-evaluating
everything, sifting though every aspect of your lives and
tossing things out: relationships, opinions, beliefs, clothes,
tastes..." My Malibu friend was born the day after I was;
she was the poster girl for major flux. I was glad to know
the planets were part of this, and I wasn't having a PTSD
relapse.

I told the psychic about the lack of physical affection
in my marriage. "But, I don't let this bother me any more,"
I added. "All marriages reach the Platonic stage. Right?"

She laid the charts on top of the Tarot cards and said,
"Look. I'm a married woman too, and I'm older than you are.
All couples need to have a good sex life. You're a Scorpio,
the sign of sex. You *have to* have orgasms."

Then she looked at the charts again. "This November,

right around your birthday, things between you and your husband will be sweet. I say that word 'sweet' because it's all I can see here. I don't know if it means you'll still be married, or not. But you probably will be. You love each other, right? That's not the problem. However, you're also going to be very depressed during that period. Not about your relationship with your husband, but something else."

I usually avoided depression by enjoying Buster. Watching his animated face and expressive body language continued to lift my spirits. When his body wriggled in a show of love, I was enchanted.

He adored going on hikes with Gracie and Reggie. They pranced through the woods with big wide smiles and wagging tails. He kept close to me on the path and no longer ran in protective circles. He seldom let himself leave my side.

He came to the barn with me and lay in his usual shady spot while he watched me ride in the arena. So he could still join me on the short trail, I often rode Scully at a walk. A house was being built at the access to that trail, and my horse froze whenever he noticed a piece of scary new construction equipment. One day, refusing to go forward, Scully tried to spin around and race back to his barn. In a calming voice, I encouraged him on. But Buster was no help at all. Instead of scampering ahead to check out the terrifying tractor or the peril-ridden pile of new lumber, he turned back and looked toward the barn too.

"You've got a point there, pal," Buster seemed to say

to Scully. "Maybe we should go back. I think that's a great idea. I'm too old for this."

Eventually, I coaxed them both to move forward.

When we rode out on the longer trails, Earl and I continued to leave Buster at home. Every few weeks another house was being built, or a new fence had blocked an access. To reach those trails, we had to ride alongside a busy paved road. Each passing car or truck was a potential danger, especially to Gracie and Reggie. We felt unsafe, and so did our horses. Riding was no longer fun. Another good thing was coming to an end.

I knew I had to put more energy into improving my marriage. I had to make some changes if our relationship was going to be "sweet" during my "depressing" birthday. A visit to my psychiatrist resulted in a prescription for a new anti-depressant with "no sexual side effects." The new drug eased my trouble with the side effects, but not with the apprehension. I was still uncomfortable when Earl touched me, and still afraid of people in motion. However, I was less afraid I might scream again. *So I scream. So what?* And I was willing to try and have fun. *Trust the Process; drum, drum, drum.* Earl deserved a partner who wanted to get out of the house.

Together, we planned a relaxing June in Quogue. We took Buster with us, hoping to have a few special weeks with him. At this point, we had very little stress in our lives. We wanted to take life slowly.

Buster was still moving slowly. The moist climate was hard on his arthritis. During our early morning walks to the

village we strolled at his pace. We had no need to hurry. We watched him scamper after an occasional deer, bird or rabbit. Close to the village, he stood still while we clipped on his leash, then he pranced toward the waiting "cookie lady."

On warmer mornings I asked him, "Do you want to stay here with me, smoochie pooch? Would you rather rest today?" His response was to run to the foyer, wriggle and squeal with excitement, then point his nose at the front door. Each evening, when the air was cool, we took him for a slow romp on the beach. Aglow with love of the moment, Earl and I held hands while we watched Buster stroll ahead of us.

Leashed dogs were welcome at our golf club, so I often took Buster with me when I practiced my swing. He lay in the shade next to the driving range and watched me hit ball after ball as I swore at myself. He didn't chase the balls, he just looked at me with concern when I was angry and smiled if I was pleased. One late afternoon, Earl met us there, hoping to play a twilight round. "Bussie can come too," he said. "It's too hot to leave him in the car."

I held Buster's leash while we played the first two holes, then I dropped it. Hanging on to it was awkward and I knew he wouldn't run away. To avoid tripping on the loose leash, he kept his back legs far apart while we all walked to the third tee box. He snorted a lot, telling me he didn't want to drag that useless leash. After watching us tee off, then walk onto the fairway, he lay down and crossed his front paws. When we called to him, he pricked his ears and looked at us, but refused to budge.

"What am I supposed to do?" his expression seemed

to ask. "I'm either on a leash, or I'm not. Make up your minds."

"Okay, B," I said to him.

We were the only people on the course; it was after six o'clock. I walked over to him and unhooked the leash. He stood up and shook his body, then smiled at me. He trotted beside me as I returned to my golf bag. While we continued playing, he stayed off the fairway, preferring to watch us from the shade. On the fourth green, he was able to step into a small pond and cool his paws.

As I was trying to putt for a very rare par, I heard Earl shouting, "Buster! No!"

When I looked up, I saw my big puppy in the middle of the pond, swimming toward a squawking duck. I was sure he wouldn't hurt the duck, and I knew how much he loved water.

"He's having fun," I said to my husband. "Let him swim." Then I putted my ball past the hole.

It had been years since I had seen Buster having so much fun. I was delighted he was doing something on his own. I wanted him to have all the fun he could have while his body still let him.

"He's scaring the duck!" Earl shouted. "She has babies."

But I was trying to focus on getting the ball in the hole. After sinking it, I walked over to the edge of the pond.

Buster was fixed on the duck, who was pretending to have a broken wing. Mother ducks do this to protect their young: if she looks like an easier catch, a predator will chase her and leave the ducklings alone.

"Sorry, Mommy duck," I said to her.

"Squawk, splash. Squawk, splash."

"Buster, come here." He kept swimming. "B, come here. Come to me." He pretended not to hear me. "Buster! Come here! Now!"

He paddled around and swam to me, then waded ashore. Big smile. Great fun.

"Good boy."

He stood next to me, then shook silty pond water all over my khakis. As we walked toward the next hole, we could hear the duck squawking again. Buster was back in the pond. I got him out, once more. We needed to talk.

"Bussie, I know you're on vacation, but you can't swim in the duck pond. You're terrorizing the poor mommy duck. I need you to stay with me, or we'll be in big trouble. They won't let me bring you here any more. That would be terrible."

He lowered his head as if to say, "Okay." Then he stayed near us the rest of the round, except to chase a goose off the fifth fairway. Those geese police instincts were still strong.

The night before we left, we all got into Earl's double scull. As usual, I held Buster against me and watched his head turn toward passing water birds. His joyful smile told me we were making a favorite memory. When we approached a friend's house for a drink, she took pictures of us arriving. We tied the boat to a ring on her bulkhead, then lifted our senior companion up to her lawn.

While we sat and talked, Buster explored the neighbors' gardens. When the daylight dimmed, we watched a slow and gentle sunset, then knew it was time for us to go.

When we arrived back in Albuquerque, Buster was very slow in the airport. *How far it is from our gate to the parking lot? Four miles?* He had never walked through an airport so slowly. I was sure his arthritis was worse, that he had to be in pain. Walking that far had become too hard for him. I started to cry. *I might never be able to take him on a plane again.* But this wasn't our last trip, I encouraged myself. In September, we were planning to take all three dogs to Quogue by car.

23

Senior Moments

The Santa Fe Opera opened on Fourth of July weekend, and I could dance with Earl during the pre-opening party. For the first time in almost five years, we danced. I was still wary of a crowded dance floor, but I could join him when the music was slow. During opera intermissions, I no longer had to stay in my seat. I could walk through crowds, cloaked in Earl's arms, as usual.

I wanted to take Buster to the ribbon-cutting ceremony for the Plaza stage. So much credit for "my" achievement belonged to him. But I really didn't need him there that day. I knew it was going to be hot and crowded; it would be hard for us to protect each other. Earl stayed behind me when we arrived, the mayor stood next to me when we each made our little speech, then we all went on to other events. I promised myself I would take Buster to the stage

another day. We deserved our special moment up there, alone.

After a few visits to the chiropractor, Buster was moving much better. Sometimes, he needed a little boost to get into my four-door sedan. When he stood by the open door and didn't jump onto the back seat, I knew he was asking me for help. So I lifted his back legs for him. Even though I was working hard to overcome my fear of being in public, I kept him with me. When I met a friend for coffee at a busy outdoor market one day, I made a point of sitting at a round table with my back to lots of foot traffic. Buster lay behind me.

While I focused on our conversation, my psychiatrist happened to walk past our table. We said hello, I introduced him to my friend, then he continued into the market. Much later, I felt a tap on my shoulder. I winced, then flinched. It was my psychiatrist.

"I'm sorry," he said. "I forgot."

"It's okay. A year ago I would have screamed."

"That's good. You're getting better."

"I am."

Buster seemed better, too. One August weekend, Earl and I rented a cabin in the Pecos Wilderness so we could have a holiday in the forest with our adorable dogs. On our second morning, we drove to the rendezvous point for a horse trip my husband had arranged. The outfitter told us we were going on a strenuous journey: six miles, each way. I was sure Buster wasn't up to that much walking, and it was too hot to leave him in the car.

"How old is he?" the outfitter asked me.

"He just turned fourteen."

"I can take him to my parents' house. They'll watch him until you get back."

I didn't want to leave Buster alone while the rest of us went off and had fun. "Thank you, but he'll find a way to go looking for us," I said. "Believe me."

The only good options were to cancel the ride or turn around if Buster was having trouble walking. Earl had gone to a lot of trouble to arrange a nice day, so we decided to try. After we mounted the horses and followed our guide up the steep, shady trailhead, I felt vexed. *If we have to turn back, we could lay Bussie across my horse's back, in front of the saddle. But, what will he do? Will he hate it? How will the horse react? I could tie him across the saddle and walk the horse.* Stop worrying until you have to, I told myself. Have fun. Trust the Process. *Trust the Universe.*

Buster was having a ball. He was romping through grassy meadows, keeping up with Gracie and Reggie, and trotting right behind our horses. After two hours of uphill riding, we stopped at a creek and ate a picnic lunch.

Just as we were bagging our litter, we heard thunder and saw lightning. Serious lightning. Going farther up the mountain wasn't safe. So we got back on the horses and turned around. On the way down we were caught in a hail-storm. Marble-sized ice balls were pelting the horses and our helmets. The horses were used to hail; we were not. Our guide led us to a grove of pine trees, where we stood under a canopy of thick branches and waited for the storm to pass. We stayed on the horses while the dogs lay down and rested. As we started back down the trail, the lush green meadows were blanketed with frozen white dots.

When we arrived at the trail base, Buster was happy

and walking very well. *Thank you, Universe. I'm sorry for all those years I doubted you. Thank you.* We opened the back of the SUV and he walked up his ramp with no effort. The next day it rained, and the dogs all napped while we read. The following day we took a short hike along a wildflower-sprinkled stream. Buster had another glorious day.

He also did well that September on the drive to Quogue. An upholsterer and I designed a thick cushion for the back of the SUV, with a groove to house his folded ramp. At each stop, after all the pups bounded out of the car for a run, Buster would walk up his ramp. When we returned to the road, he would nestle onto his cushion and sleep.

As our twenty-fifth wedding anniversary neared, Earl and I had planned a special celebration. Twenty-five years together was an achievement. Some close friends from Santa Fe came to Quogue and stayed with our dogs while we flew to Paris for the weekend. Flying from New York to Paris takes less time than flying from New Mexico to Long Island. It was a perfect opportunity.

In Paris I was able to walk through the city, but I still needed to keep my back to walls when we sat down. We strolled through neighborhoods that weren't crowded and I enjoyed it. I was having fun!

On our first night there we walked to dinner, then to the ballet at the Opera Garnier. My gift to Earl was a deep apology for so many years of being an absolute crab.

"I love you with my entire heart and soul," I told him. "I always will. I'm the luckiest woman in the world, because you love me." I meant it. *Until death do us part.* Our marriage was, indeed, becoming "sweet."

The next day, we walked through the Left Bank area,

explored two museums, then dined with Aunt Olivia. I was apprehensive about reminding her I needed my back protected, but she had selected a typical European restaurant. The seating was designed so that every woman could face the room and have her back against a wall. *Faites Confiance au processus.*

I was able to have fun in public again. I was close to being well.

When we returned to Quogue, our dogs were happy to see us, but not ecstatic. We could tell they had been indulged. "We took them for long walks on the beach," our friends told us. "They had a marvelous time, but Buster got very tired. Poor Buster. He's getting a little bit old." I hugged my darling boy and said, "Yes, he is. But aren't we all?"

A week later we had plans to go to Manhattan to visit friends and see a play. When I phoned the nice lady who baby-sits Buster during our rare day trips into the city, she was delighted to hear from me. She was wary of taking care of three dogs, but eager to see Buster again.

"How is he doing?" she asked.

"Fine. He's fourteen, but in excellent health. After his check-up in May, he was pronounced just fine. Only a little arthritis in his lower back. The vet said he and Reggie need their teeth cleaned, so we'll do that when we get home. He walks slowly now, but that's to be expected."

"I'm so glad to hear all that. The last few times I stayed with him, I gave him a hug and a kiss good-bye. I was afraid I might not see him again. It makes me sad to think of him

getting old, you know. I've spent time with a lot of people's dogs, but he's very special. There's nobody like Buster."

"Thank you. He'll be glad to see you, too."

The day before we left Quogue, Earl and I took the dogs to the beach. As usual, they bounded out of the car and the young ones raced up and down the wooden paths built to protect the dune grass. Buster stayed next to me until I told him, "Show me the way." Then he trotted ahead, relying on his front legs to get up steps. As we walked along the shore, I watched him stroll in front of us. We had no plans to return to Quogue until spring, when long walks were sure to be too hard on his arthritis. I held Earl's hand and admitted, "This is probably Buster's last walk on a beach."

I took photographs of him walking away from us, toward the setting sun. Then a few of our footprints, together in the sand. I asked Earl to take one of Buster and me sitting together, with the sea behind us.

I started crying. Buster nuzzled my face, then licked away the tears. That visit to Quogue had been a very happy time for him; I knew he didn't want me feeling sad.

We drove home on two-lane roads, through eastern mountain ranges in the peak of fall. The autumn colors were stunning, and we were able to take little hikes together each day. We all had a glorious time.

After we arrived home, Buster and I continued our visits to the chiropractor. His pace improved, and so did mine. On Halloween I scheduled his teeth cleaning, Reggie's too. The company of happy Reggie would provide him some comic relief. Blood tests were required before the

procedure, so I scheduled those also. When I spoke with the vet on the phone, I asked what more he could do for Buster's arthritis.

"Let's look at his blood tests when you come in next week," he said. "Maybe we can put him on a different pain medication. We'll see how his liver function looks."

The next week I took Reggie and Buster to the vet for their blood draws. "They're going to poke you today," I said to Buster. His soft, brown eyes looked up at me, full of questions. "Yes, it will hurt a little bit." He cocked his head and whined. "I'll be out here waiting for you, my sweetheart. You'll be fine. Everything will be okay."

The next morning, the doctor phoned with the results. "Reggie's blood results look great. But Buster's tests concern me."

"How?"

"His red blood count shows he has anemia. That might be what's making him so lethargic. He also has a high white blood cell count."

"What does that mean?"

"At this point, I can't clean his teeth. With the anemia, we can't put him under anesthesia. Why don't you bring them both in anyway? We'll clean Reggie's teeth, and take some X-rays to see what's causing Buster's anemia."

It was the day before my birthday. I hung up the phone, depressed.

24

Until....

The X-rays showed a tumor in Buster's abdomen. His system often made lipomas, benign fatty tumors. I looked at the picture of the tumor and hoped what I was seeing was another lipoma.

"This could be what's causing the anemia," the doctor said.

Earl grasped my hand.

"I'm going to refer you to a specialist in Albuquerque."

The specialist was able to see Buster that Saturday morning, at seven. My husband and I drove Buster down to the clinic. It was the longest hour drive of my life.

The doctor had the best bedside manner I have ever seen. While I sat on the floor petting Buster, he asked us about our relationship with him. We told the specialist we had adopted him from the shelter, that he had been a flying

Frisbee dog, and he had later become my service dog. It was clear he was the love of my life.

"Other than what you're here about, do you consider him a healthy dog?" he asked us.

Buster rubbed his shoulder against mine, then nudged me with his nose. "Yes," I said. "A healthy fourteen year old dog."

The doctor led us all into an exam room. He told us what was going to happen to Buster, exactly how he was going to do a biopsy of the tumor. He welcomed us to stay with Buster. Then he and a nurse lifted Buster onto a steel table and started to inject a fast-acting anesthetic.

I stroked the top of Buster's head. "This poke is going to hurt you, sweetheart. I'm sorry. That's my good boy." His legs weakened, then buckled under him. We all eased him down onto the table, and he fell asleep.

The nurse turned him over to his "white alligator" position. Then she shaved some fur off his belly. "That beautiful, white fur," the specialist said.

We all watched the monitor while the doctor moved the ultra sound wand over the tumor area. "There it is," he said. "See that black shadow next to it? It's bleeding into his stomach."

Watching his aim through the monitor, the doctor stuck a pin into the tumor, then pulled the pin out.

When Buster came to, I was holding him. He almost jumped off the table. We lifted him down to the floor, and he stood up right away.

"He's a happy camper," the doctor said. "He's in great shape." Then he asked us to follow him into his office.

"Is he in pain?" I asked him.

"It's hard to determine that. The question I like to think about is quality of life. We'll have these results on Monday night. I'll be off that day, but my partner will call you with the results."

"Then what do we do?"

"My partner usually likes to operate. He'll probably encourage you to remove the tumor. It's your decision."

"What will that entail?" Earl asked. "And will it help?"

"Some dogs live a few more years after surgery, some don't. I was about to operate on a dog last week, for the third time. He looked up at me and I could tell he was saying, 'Enough.'"

"Do you think it's cancer?" I asked him.

"I've been at this a long time. Without seeing the tests, I can't know for sure. But to me, it looks like it's probably cancer."

Tears streamed down my face. I couldn't talk anymore.

"These wonderful animals are our best friends," he continued. "The difference between them and our human friends is they don't have to suffer. We can let them die with their dignity."

"What could happen if we don't operate?" Earl asked.

I held Buster and massaged the back of his neck. *More beautiful white fur.*

"The tumor could rupture. He shouldn't run or jump anymore. But it will, eventually, burst."

"If we're careful, how long before that will happen?"

"Months. Closer to two. Not more than three." He described the visible symptoms, then said it would be fatal.

Earl was crying too.

"Think it over between now and Monday night," the doctor said. "There's nothing to decide until we know more. You can call me, any time. I'll always be available for you to talk to."

We led Buster out to the parking lot, then lifted him into the SUV. He lay down on the cushion I had designed for him, and rested. Earl and I fell into each other's arms, crying.

"I'm glad we aren't going on any trips," I said, sobbing. "I don't want to leave him."

"We're taking Cody to Costa Rica."

"Oh, dear." *I can't back out on Cody.*

"Bussie will be all right without us," Earl said. "It's only for a week."

As we drove back to Santa Fe, we were too sad to talk. All I could do was wonder what was next. *He can't go now. Buster's job isn't finished yet. I still need to get well. He promised to stay with me until I'm well. He will. I know he will. He'll be with us for Christmas.*

When we came home, Buster was still groggy from the anesthetic. Earl and I guided our sleepy puppy up his steps to the bed, then lay with him. We held him while he slept, until dark.

That night, we kept a dinner date with a retired surgeon and his wife. Buster had been to their house for dinner, and they always asked, "How's Buster?"

We told them.

"They all get tumors," the doctor said. "When they get old. They all get them."

When I described the bleeding tumor, he winced and slowly shook his head. His eyes looked sad.

"Do you think he's in a lot of pain?" I asked.

"Dogs never tell you. Unless they're yelping, they never complain. They just never do. They never complain."

As expected, the specialist's partner phoned Monday night. Earl and I both got on the phone. The biopsy report was inconclusive; he wanted us to let him operate. "We can go in, take this thing out, and it might not be cancer at all. He could be cured."

I started to feel hopeful. *We can fix this!* All night, my feelings yo-yoed from elation to dread. *What if they operate, and find cancer?*

"They'll put him to sleep," my local vet said to me on the phone the next morning.

"But I don't want our last moment to be a lie. I don't want to assure him he's going to be all right, while I watch the surgeon lead him away from me forever. If they find cancer, can we bring him back home?"

"So you can euthanize him later on? Sure. If that's what you want." Then he told me chemotherapy was an option.

"Don't do it," a friend advised me. "We did chemotherapy with one of our dogs. She was miserable. Then she died. It was awful, the whole ordeal was just awful."

I sent e-mails to my dog loving friends, "What would you do?" One replied that she had heard many stories of tumors dissolving on their own. Some expressed worries about an old dog surviving surgery, period. Another described the agony her dog endured because she kept her alive too long. None of them had faced this particular quandary. "There will be no wrong decision," someone assured

me. "Whatever you do will be the right thing." I prayed to the Universe for guidance.

I asked Cody for guidance too. We had lunch with him on his thirty-third birthday. I didn't want the occasion to be depressing, so I waited until dessert to talk about Buster. My eyes had been tearing all through the meal; Cody deserved an explanation.

"You've just been through this with someone you love," I said. "I never have. If they find cancer, should they wake him up, or not? What would you like to see done?"

"Have them keep him asleep," he said. "Don't let him suffer. Don't let him be miserable."

He reached for my hand, and held it. We both cried.

Earl and I couldn't sleep. We couldn't decide what to do. The next morning, I asked him to phone the specialist who had conducted the ultrasound. I was too convulsed with tears to talk to him.

Earl told me the details of their conversation. "He looked at the biopsy report too. He thinks it's probably cancer." Then my husband and I both came to the same, clear decision. Do nothing.

"I'm so bored," I remembered my father telling me. We were having dinner together at his favorite seaside restaurant. "I really loathe being old. There's nothing left for me to enjoy. I wake up every morning, disappointed I'm still here."

"If you're ready to go, then it's okay," I recall saying. "I'll be all right. I'll miss you terribly. But, I'll be all right."

He held my hand and said, "You mustn't miss me, Peachie. You're going to have a wonderful life."

He died of a stroke six weeks later. All in one day. No pain. There wasn't time for me to travel there; the doctors hadn't thought he was dying. I continue to miss him, every day.

"Bussie, if you want to, just go to sleep and keep on going. I'll be all right. I'll get well someday. I know you'll always take care of me, no matter where you are." He looked at me, slightly puzzled. I held my body against his, and kept stroking his chest. That white fur. "Some day, each of us will go to sleep, and never wake up. If I go first, I know you'll follow me soon. If you go first, I'll be along. I won't be very far behind you." *Please, Universe, please. Please don't let him suffer. Please don't make me call the doctor and have him put down. Please take him in his sleep. Please.*

Each morning after Earl and I made our decision, I woke up and looked down at Buster, still sleeping. His beautiful black and white body would be stretched out on his bed, right next to ours. When I stepped out of bed, he would smile at me, and I'd lie down on the floor beside him. Then, he would stretch his front legs out to me and put his paws around my neck. I'd say, "We have another day together. Oh, boy, Bussie. Another day."

Every afternoon, I'd guide him up the steps to the bed. We would cuddle for an hour or so, until he fell asleep. We cuddled a lot more now; there was always time for that. We tried to keep our lives as normal as possible. We kept his regular appointments with the chiropractor, and we saw Dr. Joe. I hadn't needed to see him since late summer; it was good to know he was still there for me.

Buster and I went to Wal-Mart and picked out a stool he could use to get into my car. After that, he would pace toward the car, step onto the stool, then ease himself onto the back seat. Very dignified. Stored at the proper angle, the stool held a water bowl he could reach while he was lying down.

I think raw liver is nauseating, but it builds red blood cells. So I bought it and cooked it for Buster very day. It seemed to make him stronger; he had a lot more energy. "My peppy puppy! My good boy."

I was sure the holidays were going to be painful for Cody. I'll always remember his girlfriend at her last Thanksgiving. So, that year, I made things very different. We had dinner with another family, in a private room at Hotel Santa Fe, the hotel our company owns. Buster was with us, resting behind my chair. The hotel staff loved him; they were delighted to see him.

Two weeks later we left for Costa Rica. While we were there I read an article about the Nobel Prize ceremony. The winner of the literature prize didn't attend. The article said she chose not to travel because she had a "social phobia." I felt sad for her. *Her phobia must be an awful form of PTSD, worse than mine.* I wondered if she had a patient and loving husband. I hoped she had a friend like Buster.

While we were away, Earl phoned our house-sitter every day for me. "Buster's fine," she told him. "I can tell he misses you, but he's doing very well. Very, very well."

Cody was doing well, too. His sense of humor was beginning to return. On our trip together, he was like a beautiful rose, opening a little more each day. He even learned to play golf. By the second day he was playing almost as well

as Earl. *The little brat!* He preferred to walk on the beach without us; he had a lot of head clearing to do. Earl and I enjoyed our private hours alone, and I learned to trust his tender touches again.

When we returned home, I continued to take Buster everywhere. A week before Christmas we went downtown. I parked the car, and we sauntered to the Plaza together. We walked up the wheelchair access ramp to the stage, then went over to its steps and sat down.

I held Buster close to me and gazed out across the Plaza. I thought about how much I had overcome since my accident, and how much stronger I was because of those struggles. The stage will always remind me of my inner strength. Buster was there through everything, leading me toward health and wisdom. *Thank you, Universe. Thank you for helping me through. Thank you for reminding me to trust you, again. Thank you for giving Buster to me. Thank you for all the time we've had together. Thank you for this moment.*

Scurrying children squealed and giggled behind us. They darted back and forth across the stage's hardwood floor, then up and down the ramp. Families love to play on the stage. During the summer there is a free concert every night. Now, people talk about the "gazebo" or "bandstand" as if it's always been there.

While I held Buster, he was watching people and their dogs walking across the Plaza. Always alert, he was still taking care of me. We walked back down the ramp, then ambled to the car. His pace was very slow.

Three days before Christmas, I went to K-Mart. I didn't have an important errand; I just needed a little chain to finish fixing a necklace. I left Buster in the car because the

walk to the store was too long for him. I remembered how tired I felt after my accident, when walking from my car to a store was exhausting. "I'll be right back, sweetie. I won't be in the store very long. Have a good little nap."

I strolled through the busy store without feeling stressed. I walked around the jewelry counter, my back to other shoppers every minute. Christmas crowds? They didn't bother me. *I must be well now.*

I drove to another crowded store and enjoyed buying something there too. *I can't believe this. I can shop in crowded stores by myself, three days before Christmas. I must be well. I can go anywhere I want to, now. I feel so free! He promised. He promised to stay with me until...*

On Christmas Eve, I sat on our living room floor with Buster. Earl and I lit candles with Cody, thankful for another year together. While I focused on my son, Buster lay on his back. He smiled at me, and let me stroke his chest. The fur on his belly had almost grown back.

During the days after Christmas, Buster would be right next to my desk, sleeping on the floor. Sometimes he would stir and look up to make sure I was still there. He would see me, then smile. Then he would "huff" to me, and I would answer back. After that, he would tuck himself into a more comfortable position and sigh himself back into a deep sleep.

Our Epilogue

When Buster left my side, the year was almost over. The day before, he wouldn't eat or drink, except to sip water from the palm of my hand. Near midnight Earl and I found him outside, lying still, breathing heavily, not sleeping. It was pouring rain, cold enough to snow, so we brought him inside and closed the dog flap. When I lay on his dog bed, next to my wet puppy, he got up and plopped down on the other side of the bedroom.

Knowing he was suffering, I tried to get some sleep. *Maybe he'll be better in the morning.* I hoped he would stop panting; I wanted him to rest. *Rest, my love. Rest in peace.*

By dawn, the rain had stopped. But I found Buster lying next to the kitchen door, still panting. When I opened the door, he wouldn't stand up to go outside. I knelt next to him and asked, "What do you want to do, my friend?" He looked at me with sad eyes while I stroked the top of his head. Then I realized he had already told me, he had gone out into the cold rain to die.

I waited for the animal clinic to open, then phoned them. "It's time," I said to the doctor. He promised to come

to our house at eleven. Earl and I carried Buster away from the door and laid him next to the fireplace. We took turns petting him and telling him we loved him, never letting him lie there alone. "I love you, my angel," I said to Buster. The doctor will be here soon. He'll take your pain away. You'll never ever suffer again. I promise."

I remembered the pleas I had made to the Universe. *Please don't let me have to put him down.* I had never wanted to cause his death, or deceive him about what the doctor's injection would do to him. But, it was clear he wanted his suffering to end.

For once, Gracie, Wrex and Reggie didn't ask for their share of our affection. Gracie sniffed at Buster's abdomen, wrinkled her nose, and moved away. Reggie and Wrex kept their distance too. As Earl and I sat holding Buster, his breathing became heavier.

"Go my darling. Go," I whispered. "I know you'll always be with me. I won't be very far behind you. Show me where we're all supposed to go. Show me the way."

"Fly, Bussie, fly," Earl said. "Soar high into the air and catch that Frisbee."

As we stroked him, he heaved a deep cough. Then he put his head down, and I felt his breathing stop. "Good boy. That's my good boy. I love you, my angel. I always will."

The next day was New Year's Eve. I bought four helium-filled balloons, two white and two black. Just before sunset, Earl and I went out into the garden and held the balloons high. We cried as we let their strings slip out of our fingers. We watched the black and white bouquet sail

up and away from us, far into the evening sky. When it had gone too far for us to see, I buried my face against my husband's chest and howled. He held me in his loving arms until I was ready to start letting go.

Buster's Glossary

Licking his "chops": I want a treat.
Rolling over on his back, so he looks like a white alligator:
 pet me NOW
A slight stroke on a door: Are you in there?
Lots of squealing: I'm delighted!
A little squeal: What do you mean?
A soft growl: Don't do that.
A subtle snarl: I said, don't do that.
A curled lip: Go away.
A series of whining talking sounds: Listen to me.
A nudge of his nose under one's hand: Come with me
 and….
A series of hops, his torso and nose pointing away: Come
 this way, hurry!
Three hard pants: I'm right here.
Several pants, in the back seat of the car: Open the
 window.
A big yawn, with a little whine at the end: "Hello."

Buster's Rules

Give me a job, or I'll find other work.

Amuse me, or I'll find someone who will.

I'll lick your face a lot more if you're wearing my favorite cream.

When in bed, pet me when my head is facing you, and don't stop.

If I'm facing the foot of the bed, don't move.

Pills must be given to me with cheese or ground meat.

If I'm pretending not to hear you, your request isn't granted.

Take me with you.

Don't tie me to anything.

I'll only "stay" if I can still see you.

Leave me in the car, or I'll come and look for you.

Never lie to me.

More About Post-Traumatic Stress Disorder

Over seven million Americans suffer from PTSD. Many more may not know they have the disease. It can result from war, death of a loved one, injury and mental or emotional trauma. I'm not an expert on this disease, but I feel sad for people who are trapped in it. My symptoms were mild, compared to what others have been known to experience. Health care professionals are more aware of the disease today, and can provide treatment. Helpful information about diagnosis and treatments can be found on the Internet. Here is a list of some of the symptoms:

Nightmares
Flashbacks
Persistent daily thoughts
 about traumatic events
Persistent memories of
 those events
Emotional numbness
Trouble feeling affectionate

Startling easily
Irritability
Aggression
Sleeplessness
Gaining or losing weight
Depression

More About Service Dogs

There are many types of assistance dogs, including service dogs, guide dogs, hearing dogs and therapy dogs. There is a great deal of information about them on the Internet, including schools where service dogs can be trained or purchased. There is a school in almost every state in the country. I suggest contacting these organizations:

Delta Society: The National Service Dog Center: www.deltasociety.org

International Society of Service Dog Partners: www.iaadp.org

Keystone Human Services: www.keystonehumanservices.org

Guiding Eyes for the Blind: www.guidingeyes.org

Acknowledgements

I would like to thank some of Buster's friends. They helped him live a long and happy life: Earl Potter, Cody Potter, Gracie Potter, Reggie Potter, Wrex Potter, Thundercloud Potter, Scully, Corey and Snip; Jacques and Patrice; Joe Veltmann, Meesha Veltmann and Maggie Woods; Michael Dudelczyk; Karen Kleinfelter; Bill Smythe; Diane Polss; Cathy Caballerro, Bob Carmichael, Valentine Carmichael, Rell Carmichael, Rugby Carmichael, Patti Carmichael and Bosco; Stephanie Daniel; Cheryl Murchy; Ann Dozier; Randal Kleiser; Nancy Perlman; Jered Barclay; Patrick and Susan Farrow; Mary and Bill Kerr; Tom and Nan Rees, Chloe Rees and Luke Rees; Charlotte Lander; Esteban Armendariz; Dr. Tom; Carole and Fred Bennett; Lisa Bracken and Lilly Bracken; Clare Thaw; Joan Bokum; Sharon Schenck; Susie Dubin, Ron Dubin, Heather Dubin, Jo Jo Dubin and Betty Dubin; John Tishman, Tex Tishman and Tad Tishman; Russell Hayes, Mary Kane Hayes, and Daisy Hayes; Diane Bucallo; Barbara Metcalf, Valentine, Keith and Valerie; The Hilton brothers; Kathy Trager; Wendy and Stanley Marsh; Michael Marsh; Ken Parmalee,

Carole Parmalee, Chilie Parmalee and Skye Parmalee; Beth Longanecker and Naiomi Longanecker; Kenny Laymon and Harley Laymon; Gail Roos, Cricket Roulette and Moochie Roulette; Bill Fine; Doug McLeod, Lou McLeod, Cowboy McLeod, Sugar McLeod, Nacho McLeod, Happy and Homer; Carter and Thea Beckett; Cordelia Ornelas; Vi Ortiz; Rebecca Trujillo; Jim Bagby; Paul Margetson; David Ortiz; Blaire Bennett; the Colin family; John Sandoval; Caroline Stevenson; Amelia Martinez; Ruth Wilson; Diane Hautmann; Brent and Missy Lynch; Marcia Bradley; Colette and Pam; Fay Harbach; Eva Wylie; Sue Clarke and Chelsea Clarke; Winifred Braden, who wasn't fond of dogs; Robert Osborne and Dr. Dave Gonzales.

And my special thanks to a few who only met him in words. They've helped me keep his memory alive: Jim Smith, Carl Condit, Sandi Gelles-Cole, Helen Zimmerman, Sally Arteseros, Marilyn J. Mason, Ph.D.; Sylvia Chase and Dominick Dunne.

www.ingramcontent.com/pod-product-compliance
Lightning Source LLC
Chambersburg PA
CBHW031432270326
41930CB00007B/667

* 9 7 8 1 6 3 2 9 3 0 3 8 5 *